FOR LOVE OF MY PEOPLE I
WILL NOT REMAIN SILENT

JOSEPH CARDINAL ZEN

For Love of My People I Will Not Remain Silent

A Series of Eight Lectures in
Defense and Clarification of the
2007 Letter of Pope Benedict XVI
to the Church in the People's
Republic of China

Translated by Pierre G. Rossi

IGNATIUS PRESS   SAN FRANCISCO

Italian edition:
Per amore del mio popolo non tacerò:
Ricordando il decimo anniversario della Lettera
di Papa Benedetto alla Chiesa in Cina
Choralife Publications, Hong Kong, 2018

Published in 2019 by Ignatius Press, San Francisco
ISBN 978-1-62164-314-2
Library of Congress Control Number 2018965658
Printed in the United States of America ∞

CONTENTS

INTRODUCTION

by Aurelio Porfiri

This text contains a series of lectures that Joseph Cardinal Zen delivered in Hong Kong to commemorate the tenth anniversary of Pope Benedict XVI's 2007 Letter to the Church in the People's Republic of China. The lectures were in Chinese and then translated into Italian by the Cardinal himself, with the assistance of some native speakers. The tone is that of a lecture—that is, informal, which makes the reading more interesting and informative.

I met Joseph Cardinal Zen many years ago. For family reasons, I developed a strong relationship with the people of Hong Kong in 2000, almost twenty years ago. At the time, the Bishop of Hong Kong was John Cardinal Baptist Wu Cheng-chung, and his Coadjutor Bishop was Joseph Zen. Bishop Zen succeeded to Cardinal Wu in 2002 (and remained in this position until 2009). When reading newspapers and talking with people at that time, I learned of Cardinal Zen's strong opposition to the Chinese government and their policies. I met him in Rome, when he was already Bishop of Hong Kong. I remember meeting him and experiencing his anger because of the behavior of the Chinese government against religion, especially the government's repressions and persecutions.

From 2008 to 2015 I had the occasion to live in Macau and work there. I have to say that I was influenced negatively about Cardinal Zen, who was portrayed to me as an obstacle between China and the Holy See. Thankfully, I learned later that I was wrong and repented in time, understanding that the real obstacle for the reconciliation between the Holy See and the Chinese government was the ideology behind the government: Communism, which wherever applied has always persecuted religions.

But let us go back a few months, around June 2018. During the recent years, I became a good friend with the Cardinal, so every time I visited Hong Kong I had dinner with him or met him for a chat. We also wrote a little book together in Italian, *L'agnello e il dragone: Dialoghi su Cina e Cristianesimo* (The lamb and the dragon: Dialogues on China and Christianity; Chorabooks, 2016), where the Cardinal also talked of his life and ideas. During one of our meetings, in June if I remember correctly, the Cardinal mentioned to me that he was revising a series of conferences given in Hong Kong about the Pope's Letter to Chinese Catholics. The conferences, given in Chinese, presented the history and development of this document by Benedict XVI. So these conferences were written by a key witness, Cardinal Zen, who was involved in the preparation of the Letter. He was thinking of collecting all the conferences in a book. It happens that I have a small publishing company, which has already published books from outstanding writers, so of course I offered to publish the book in Italian. We were able to publish the book, one or two days before the date of the signing of the agreement (that was not revealed until the very moment of the signing, so we were really lucky to be able to achieve that). So the book was written prior to the provisional agreement; but it is very important to understand why that provisional agreement is not a good move. It is important to understand the background of the relationship between China and the Vatican in the last decades, and what the expectations are of the two sides; especially important is why the Letter of Benedict XVI was in the end not fully understood and implemented. The book has had many reviews in the Italian press and from important Catholic-oriented blogs, such as *La Nuova Bussola Quotidiana*, *Duc in Altum*, and *Stilum Curiae*. So we desired to have an English version because of the importance of the topics discussed. Read the book, make your assessment of the issues here described, and see if you do or do not share Cardinal Zen's assessement, which is mine as well.

EVENTS BEFORE AND AFTER THE ILLEGITIMATE ORDINATION ATTEMPT AND CANONIZATION PROTEST IN 2000

First Lecture
June 19, 2017

This is the tenth anniversary of the Letter of Pope Benedict XVI to the Church in the People's Republic of China.[1] The Letter was a precious gift that we must appreciate and remember. Let us also pray for the Pope Emeritus, that the Lord may grant him a long life.

This is the first of eight lectures that will present the precedents and issues connected to the

---

[1] Letter of the Holy Father Pope Benedict XVI to the Bishops, Priests, Consecrated Persons, and Lay Faithful of the Catholic Church in the People's Republic of China (May 27, 2007).

Letter, so that it can be understood better and appreciated more.

Pope Benedict XVI

Pope Benedict XVI, the former Cardinal Rat-zinger, is certainly qualified to write such a Letter, due to his experience of totalitarian regimes, first Nazism and then Communism. Thus, he could understand well the situation of a Church under a regime like that of the People's Republic of China. (Pope Benedict was born in 1927. When Nazism took over in 1933, he was six years old and lived under Nazi control until he was eighteen. Afterward, Germany was divided into West and East Germany, with the eastern part under the control of the Communists until 1990.)

Our high-ranking Vatican officials, most of whom are Italian, have not lived under such a totalitarian regime. This kind of a blessing, however, means that they have not had any direct experience under a totalitarian regime, and so their concept of it is somewhat naïve and optimistic.

In addition to Pope Benedict's childhood experience regarding such regimes, he had the opportunity of learning about the Church in China when he was the Prefect of the Congregation for the Doctrine of the Faith (CDF). He took part in the meetings convened by the Congregation for the Evangelization of Peoples (CEP), with Prefect Cardinal Tomko, especially a final "secret meeting" on October 4, 2000.[2]

Cardinal Tomko

Who is Cardinal Tomko? What has he done? How did those meetings go?

It is common knowledge that the Communist Party took power in China in 1949 and that it set up the Chinese Patriotic Catholic Association (CPCA) in 1957. The following year it began ordaining Bishops without a mandate from the Holy See. The years of the Cultural Revolution (1966–1976) were a time when every religion disappeared. After this, when leader Deng Xiaoping began a policy of openness, a new scenario unfolded. Before we had what was called the "bamboo curtain", which hermetically sealed China from the rest of the world. Almost nothing was known about China. With the policy of openness, things changed. At the time, Cardinal Tomko, who is Czechoslovak and thus knows

---

[2] The events that led to this meeting are discussed below, in the section about the illegitimate ordination attempt and the canonization protest in the year 2000.

the Communists well, used to convene so-called secret meetings to face this new situation and to which he applied all his experience and wisdom.

"Secret meetings"

When China began opening up, the Cardinal started getting a lot of news. To put these to better use, he began organizing meetings every one to two years to study how to use this precious information. The two dicasteries in charge of the affairs of the Church in China, namely, the Secretariat of State and the CEP, took part in such events, through the Secretary of State—the Secretary of the Secretariat, who is an Archbishop and serves as the Minister of Foreign Affairs of the Holy See—and the Deputy Secretary, a Monsignor who serves as the Deputy Minister of Foreign Affairs in charge of negotiations when these are possible. The CEP was represented by its Prefect, Secretary, and Under-Secretary. Experts were invited from other dicasteries, like the Prefect of the CDF, Cardinal Ratzinger, since often, issues had to be dealt with from the point of view of the doctrine of the Faith, as for example, the validity of episcopal ordinations. Finally, some Bishops and experts from Hong Kong, Taiwan, and Macau were invited. But they were not that many. The commission for the Church in China did not exist yet. Only these "secret meetings" were held.

I too had the opportunity of taking part. First, I was the president of the Association of Major Religious Superiors of Hong Kong. I then visited China, where some of my confreres lived. In 1989, I began teaching in various seminaries in China (without asking the Holy See for its permission, but, once they heard about it, they encouraged me).

Teaching in seminaries, of the official Church, of course, gave me the opportunity of learning about many things that I could not imagine before, good things and less good things. The "less good things" include the terrible control by the Communist government. The "good things" include the fact that there was faithfulness not only within the underground Church, but also among most people in the official Church. We came to realize that our categories were too sharply divisive, when in reality there were so many healthy forces.

Every time I came back after months of teaching in China, I reported to my Superior General. These reports were also passed on to the Holy See—that is, to Cardinal Tomko (the information was very useful to the Holy See). As a result of our frequent encounters during these meetings,

Cardinal Tomko was getting to know me better and ended up suggesting my name as Coadjutor Bishop of Hong Kong, and as such I continued to attend these meetings.

Some say that there was some friction between the Secretariat of State and the CEP because the Secretariat of State tends to be friendly with governments, while the CEP is more cautious in its defense of the Church. However, in the years of Cardinal Tomko, the two sides came close to each other and understood each other well on how to help both the official community and the underground community in China.

No official negotiations were underway between the Holy See and the Chinese government, but the Under-Secretary of the Secretariat of State sometimes tried to hold some unofficial talks, as when, on his way to North Korea, he stopped in Beijing to see if his counterpart might agree for a chat. These talks could also be quite detailed, and this Monsignor Under-Secretary referred everything to us in those secret meetings.

The so-called eight points

In 1988, with fresh knowledge about the situation, the CEP saw fit to issue some instructions on how to behave within the Church in China:

the so-called eight points. The *first point* clearly confirms the principle that the Catholic Church must always be united with the Pope. The *second point* notes that, since 1957, the government uses the CPCA to control the Church: this association is not acceptable to us.

The *third point* concerns the ordination of illegitimate Bishops, which began in 1958. How can this problem be solved? First of all, are these ordinations valid? After a serious study by the CDF, obviously under Cardinal Ratzinger, it was concluded that there are no reasons to say that they are invalid; that is, although illegitimate, they were valid. Consequently, the priests ordained by these Bishops were also validly ordained and their Masses were also true Masses. So what should the faithful do? According to the *fourth point*, the faithful must, first of all, seek out good priests—that is, those who do not support the CPCA; however, if in case of difficulties, like the danger of being arrested, and one has a strong desire to receive the sacraments, he could also turn to other priests. The traditional principle of the Church is that the faithful have the right to receive valid sacraments, but at the same time they must avoid bad example and also the danger, for instance, of being forced to join the CPCA. In short, the faithful must exercise their rights with great caution. The *fifth point* concerns the *communicatio in sacris*—that is, concelebration. On this point, the Holy See was very cautious. When priests from the official community travel outside of China, they are not to be invited to concelebrate. They can celebrate the Mass in private. When foreign priests travel to China, they too must not concelebrate with priests who are members of the CPCA.

The *sixth point* amazed us. The Church needs to train seminarians. In 1988, several seminaries belonging to the official community were already open. The underground community had also tried to open seminaries, but that was a very difficult thing to do. The sixth point says that when the underground community has seminarians and is unable to train them, it can send them to the seminaries of the official community. We wondered how we could be sure that the seminaries of the official community were good enough. Obviously, in individual cases we must make sure that this condition exists. Given this instruction from the Holy See, many of us in Hong Kong and Taiwan decided to go to teach in the seminaries of the official community. We were a little hesitant, but eventually the facts comforted us. Given the occasion, I asked Cardinal Tomko how he could take such a bold decision and issue this sixth point. He answered that it was his experience that priests who are trained in the seminaries under the control of the Communists are the most rebellious against the Communist government. It means that the Lord is enlightening them.

The last two points, *seventh* and *eighth*, concern donating books and other items. In this area, there was a need to be cautious to avoid making mistakes, despite one's good will.

To sum up, we can say that the eight points show an attitude of somewhat stringent caution, which, in actual situations, can be practiced within a broad understanding.

Strategy of broad tolerance on the part of the Holy See

Since many were going to China—for example, the Franciscans went to visit their confreres—they brought out messages. The Franciscan Dong Guang-qing, an illegitimate Bishop, asked for the Holy See's forgiveness because he had accepted the illegitimate ordination under severe pressure. Now, he hoped that the Holy Father could forgive him, and he promised that he would be a good Bishop. So Pope John Paul II ordered Cardinal Tomko to investigate the case, to make sure that he was a worthy and zealous person. It is understandable that when these Bishops are legitimized, they and their people are very happy. What is more, young Bishops chosen by the government were brave enough to ask for permission from the Pope, promising that without the Pope's permission they would not accept the ordination. Also in such cases, the Pope would order an investigation and, after verification, would approve the ordinations. All this went on, providing many with a great sense of consolation.

Did the government know any of this? Of course *it did*—even if our people tried to do everything in secret. So why didn't the government react forcefully? Since everything was done quietly, it was not causing the government to lose face, and so it tolerated it. But when the government realized that so many Bishops now followed the Pope, it turned to the use of force. Thus, two things happened in 2000.

The year 2000: An illegitimate ordination attempt and a canonization protest

On January 6 of the year 2000, while Pope John Paul II ordained twelve Bishops in Rome, Beijing planned to carry out the illegitimate ordination of twelve Bishops. It did not, however, fully succeed. Only five showed up, while the other seven were nowhere to be seen. Even the seminarians at the national seminary, who were supposed to serve in the ceremony, boycotted it. Obviously, they were punished for this; that is, they were expelled from the seminary. The Bishop of Xi'an, Monsignor Li Du'an, was among those who showed courage and refused to take part in the illegitimate ordination.

In March of that year, the Pope approved the canonization of the Blessed Martyrs in China. This came about as a result of the efforts of Cardinal Shan of Taiwan, who pointed out to Pope John Paul II that the martyrs of Japan, Korea, Thailand, and Vietnam had been canonized, but not those of China. The Pope ordered the start of the procedures, but with great caution. Thus, the list of the canonized ends at the year 1930, so as not to arouse suspicions among Chinese Communists that any of the martyrs persecuted by them would be canonized. When the decision to canonize was made public, there was no strong reaction on the part of the government in Beijing. However, as October 1 approached, a great campaign against canonization was launched with all the Bishops called to Beijing to protest with a letter to the Pope against the glorification of people seen as "imperialists". Under great pressure, many Bishops signed the letter. Once again, Monsignor Li Du'an went missing at the time. While he is always humble and compliant, especially with local government officials, he becomes very courageous when it comes to fundamental principles. This time, the government decided to punish him. No one was allowed to teach in his seminary anymore, a punishment that hurt especially hard since the seminary was what he cherished the most. But his conscience would not allow him any other course. He is indeed a great Bishop!

It is obvious that this led to a situation of conflict. The canonization was held on October 1. A "secret meeting" was held on October 4, the last one under Cardinal Tomko. Cardinal Ratzinger was present; given his exceptional memory, he certainly kept in mind the situation of the Church in China.

Under Church rules, Church officials retire at the age of seventy-five. Thus, Cardinal Tomko had to retire in 2002. Unfortunately, his young and inexperienced successor did very little for the Church in China during his five-year term: no meetings. The two officials in the CEP with expertise on the Church in China were fired: one from the Society of the Divine Word who had lived in Beijing for many years, and a PIME (Pontifical Institute for Foreign Missions) missionary who had spent many years in Hong Kong.

Cardinal Tomko promoted a policy of broad tolerance. His successor continued along the same path, but with a difference. Cardinal Tomko moved cautiously and conducted necessary inquiries; when there was also an underground Bishop, the one from the official community was legitimized as an Auxiliary Bishop, even if for the government he was the only Bishop. Under Tomko's successor, some of the Bishops ordained on January 6, 2000, were too easily legitimized. That ordination was not like previous ones. It was a clear challenge to the Pope's authority. There was also not as much pressure as before. We know that the seven who did not participate were not severely punished. In short, those five years were rather blank; in reality, things went backward.

The year 2005: Death of a Pope

After a long pontificate, Pope John Paul II left this world on April 2, 2005. Heads of state were invited to his funeral. Since Taiwan had diplomatic relations with the Vatican, Taiwanese President Chen Shui-bian came. After years of impasse, the government of mainland China also thought of sending a delegation, seeing it as an opportunity for an overture. But upon learning of the presence of Taiwan's president, it decided not to participate. The Holy See (somewhat unreasonably) asked Chen Shui-bian not to participate in Pope Benedict's inaugural ceremony.

No Chinese delegation showed up on that occasion either. Nonetheless, since they were still in Rome, the Holy See tried to be very kind toward them by taking them, for example, to the Vatican museums on a day that they were closed. Clearly, this was the start of a dialogue of sorts.

Realizing the start of the dialogue, I was very much worried. The Secretary of State had said: "Our Nunciature in Taiwan is the Nunciature to China; if Beijing agrees, we could move it to Beijing. I don't mean tomorrow; I mean even tonight." The Prefect of the CEP was still the same young Cardinal. Can they conduct any good negotiations?

In November of the year 2005, I was in Rome for the meetings of the post-synodal council.[3] I wrote a letter to Pope Benedict, expressing my concerns: the two Holy See officials in charge did not seem to me to be up to the hard task. I waited for an answer, concerned that the letter might have ended up in the hands of one of the two. After my seven-page letter of November, I received a Christmas card, one of those folded greeting cards with an image on the outside, a few words in Latin, with the (small) signature of Pope Benedict on the inside. There were also some

[3] Synod of Bishops, XI Ordinary General Assembly, "The Eucharist: Source and Summit of the Life and Mission of the Church".

(seemingly printed) lines in small characters that I thought might be a quote from the Bible. I didn't even try to read it; my only thought was, Why doesn't the Pope write to me, even a few words, saying that he had received the letter?

The year 2006: Elevated to the College of Cardinals

At the end of January 2006, before going back again to Rome for some meetings, I cleaned out my desk and came across the Christmas card. I tried to read the small print. They were not printed words, but handwritten by the Pope, thanking me for my long letter. He wrote that he appreciated my zeal for the Church in China. In February of the same year, news came that the Pope was going to give me the Cardinal's biretta.

In China, an announcement appeared in the paper *Fides* that the Pope was going to appoint twelve Cardinals. Full stop. No nationality was mentioned, much less that one of them would be Chinese. The Chinese government was obviously unhappy at the news and banned priests and nuns from sending greetings to me. Of that, Mr. Liu Bainian (vice chairman of the CPCA) said that if all the Bishops were like me, then China would become like Poland.

A large group accompanied me to Rome. Thus, the flag with the five stars flew in St. Peter's Square. My heart obviously was all for the Church in China. That day I went to Vatican Radio to celebrate Mass for my brothers in China. As I was going, I met with Pope Benedict, who gave me the task of giving a special blessing to those faithful. During the Mass, I told my brothers and sisters in China that I had received the scarlet vestment in their name because it represented the red of the blood of the martyrs.

On that day, I sent a note to the Chinese embassy in Italy, asking them if I could meet with the ambassador. They told me that he was in Beijing. At least I showed some courtesy to them.

Difficult beginning for the pontificate of Pope Benedict

Although Pope Benedict worked for many years in the Holy See helping Pope John Paul II as Prefect of the CDF, he encountered many difficulties at the start of his Petrine office. Among Curia officials, he was not considered "one of them" (in fact, the building of the Secretariat of State and the building of the CDF are on opposite ends of St. Peter's Basilica). In the Secretariat of State, especially, many are Italians, while Pope

Benedict was a foreigner. Even the new Secretary of State, appointed by Pope Benedict, although Italian, was considered a "foreigner" and had to wait a year before his predecessor moved out of the office and flat. All this I am saying might seem like gossip, but if I mention it, it is because I want people to understand that the Church too is made up of men and that Pope Benedict encountered difficulties.

The Pope sent the Prefect for the CEP to Naples as Archbishop. As his successor, he invited an Indian Cardinal, someone who had worked for many years in the department of foreign affairs, had been Apostolic Nuncio several times, and later served as the Archbishop of Mumbai—that is, someone highly qualified for such a job.

When Pope Benedict made me a Cardinal, I realized that he wanted me to help him with the Church in China, but to have that confirmed, I asked for a short audience in September. Once I had that confirmation, I thought it necessary to inform the new Prefect of the CEP. As soon as he saw me, he said: "Don't fret too much; the Lord has time." I answered him, saying, "Yes, the Lord has time, but we can also be impatient; so many years have gone by." I told him that I liked Psalm 44, which we priests recite every two weeks in the Breviary, a Psalm that ends with: "Rise up, come to our help! Deliver us for the sake of your merciful love!" (v. 26). He told me: "Cardinal Zen, don't forget that the Communists are also our brothers; our Lord died on the Cross for them." And I replied, "But, Your Eminence, do you think I don't believe in what you are saying? However, if the Communists are my brothers, so are the Bishops that they jail. On which side should I stand?" He ended the conversation saying: "There are many things that we can do but you cannot." In short, he wanted me to stay out of it. My answer was: "Yes. You can make more mistakes; we can't."

What this meeting proves is that there was no possibility of collaboration. He certainly deserves a lot of credit for what he did in his career, but he also had his limits. He had too many illusions about the Ostpolitik of his mentor, Cardinal Casaroli.

Many things happened in the year 2006. At the end of April and in early May, two illegitimate episcopal ordinations took place. Since the new officials had not yet taken up their office, I think the Pope himself was behind the strict statement that mentioned the principle of excommunication as envisaged by canon law in such cases. Initially, it appeared that the statement had had some effect, but in November, another illegitimate ordination took place. I thought that we had to examine how to stop such ordinations.

I informed the Secretary of State and the Prefect of the CEP: "Toward the end of December, I am coming to Rome and I hope to meet Your Eminences." They replied saying: "We are very busy." I wrote back: "It doesn't matter. I'll be in Rome for three days. You can call me at any time, day or night." When I was in Rome, they didn't call me. What could I do? Ask to see the Pope? I decided to write him a letter with copies for the two Cardinals, and then left for Hong Kong for Christmas. In the letter, I wrote, among other things: "The underground community is very worried and discouraged. I hope the Pope can say a few words of encouragement, for example, during the Christmas celebrations." After Christmas Day, I wanted to see if the Pope had said something. I found nothing. After the second day, the feast day of Saint Stephen, I tried again and found nothing. However, someone told me: "There is a report in the *South China Morning Post* about the Holy Father saying something during the Angelus on Saint Stephen's Day." I checked it out, and to my great consolation I saw that the Holy Father had used words from my letter to encourage the faithful in China: "We must not be discouraged even if everything at present seems to be a failure because suffering for the Lord is always a victory." Let me point out that the two Cardinals also saw that the Holy Father had backed my position. Yes, after the Christmas of the Lord there is the Christmas of Saint Stephen because the death of the martyr is his birth in Heaven.

In this first lecture, I have revealed some of the background and presented some important figures. In doing so, I wanted to help everyone to understand the circumstances in which Pope Benedict wrote his Letter to the Church in China. It is in this difficult situation that he sought to help the Church there.

I could not avoid talking a bit about myself—that is, of my relationship with Pope Benedict. I can truly testify that he is a Pope who loves China. From our relationship also comes a certain special duty for me to explain his Letter.

2

EVENTS SHORTLY BEFORE AND AFTER THE LETTER

Second Lecture
June 20, 2017

The meeting of February 2007

In February 2007, a few years after his election (2005), Pope Benedict convened a meeting like those that Cardinal Tomko organized periodically—that is, a "joint" meeting (with top officials from the Secretariat of State and the CEP) that included others (i.e., Bishops and experts from Hong Kong, Macau, and Taiwan). After Cardinal Tomko's retirement, such meetings were no longer held, but for Pope Benedict, they were very useful.

Main goal of the meeting: Discuss the plan of a Letter to the Church in China

The main goal of the meeting was to help the Pope write a Letter to the Church in the People's Republic of China. The Holy See had already prepared a draft Letter in 2002. The Holy See had held consultations on such a draft. I too was consulted on the matter. However, a majority was not in favor of a Letter by the Holy See. The atmosphere was tense, and there was concern that each party would have done whatever they wanted with the Letter. Since the Letter had to be fair, each party could find something that proved them right. However, this would not solve any of the problems.

The draft was quite good. Now that the Pope wanted to write the Letter, we were confident that it would have been received with reverence, also because the atmosphere was better than in 2002. Hence, in accordance with the Pope's wishes, we began to express our suggestions on how to improve the draft Letter.

Three things discussed at the meeting

First thing: an advance Letter to the Bishops in China. The draft Letter from 2002 was addressed to the Bishops; the Pope now wanted to address

it to the Bishops, priests, nuns, and the faithful—
that is, everybody. Those present at the meeting
thought that it would be a good idea to write
a Letter to the Bishops before releasing the Pope's
Letter, so that they could prepare themselves to
join together and stand courageously on the side
of the Pope's Letter. Unfortunately, the Holy See
in the end did not write any advance Letter.

Second thing: in the case of illegitimate episcopal
ordinations, canon 1382 envisages the excommunication for the ordained and those who ordain.
But Mr. Liu Bainian is a layman and does not fall
under canon law. Yet, he was de facto the one
who promoted and organized everything. Under
the circumstances, it was proposed to impose
upon him a canonical penalty for promotion of
schism. Someone then said that perhaps it is better
to admonish him first; if he continues, then the
penalty would follow. Everyone agreed that this
was a reasonable proposal. Finally, someone said
that perhaps it was better to wait until the Pope's
Letter comes out first and then admonish Mr. Liu
Bainian. This was agreed at the meeting, but was
later completely forgotten.

Third thing, also important: that of the privileges
in times of emergency (violent persecution). This
refers especially to the power to ordain Bishops
and only afterward inform the Holy See. When
a Bishop knows he is about to be arrested, he can

ordain a successor, sometimes even the successor of his successor. This is necessary when it is not possible to communicate with the Holy See. But in 2007 the situation was already different, with easier communications. This power no longer seemed necessary (even though nothing untoward had occurred when this power was exercised, while it is known that unseemly cases occurred in Catholic communities in Central Europe under Communism). But there were also other powers—for example, the dispensation to ordain a priest without proper training. Other minor powers, for example, regarded the use of oil on Holy Thursday. It was agreed that the CEP would draw up a list of the powers that had been revoked and those still in force. However, it was then said that answers would be provided when they were interrogated on individual subjects. No list was drawn up.

Someone insisted on the advisory nature of the meeting. However, not heeding the three decisions is a sign of little respect on the part of the Roman Curia for the participants in this important meeting.

Two significant facts before the publication of the Pope's Letter

Before the publication of the Letter we must note two marginal things that deserve to be mentioned.

34

At the end of March, an article appeared in the English edition of UCAN (Union of Catholic Asian News). There are strong reasons to believe that it was written by a priest in China and translated into English by someone else. I found it dangerous. Its central idea was that the problems between the Church in China and the government are essentially misunderstandings, so it was hoped that the Pope's Letter would not exacerbate these misunderstandings; therefore, the important thing was to show magnanimity. This is like saying that the Pope must not speak on the big principles. Now this is dangerous. In fact, both the draft and our discussions and finally the Pope's Letter clearly deal with the doctrinal principles that are the basis of any truly constructive dialogue. At the end of April, I wrote an article for *Kung Kao Po*, Hong Kong's Catholic paper, saying that we must expect the Pope's Letter to provide clear guidelines to follow.

The other fact, in mid-May, was a statement by the Secretary of State: "The Pope's Letter has been definitively approved." Don't you find this sentence strange? The Pope's Letter was "approved". By whom? By the Pope? Shouldn't it have said that the Pope had finished writing the Letter? Still, the sentence portrays something that we could only suspect—namely, that even in the final stretch, Curia officials were still able to present their suggestions, for which they needed the Pope's approval. Such an opportunity was not afforded to us.

The Letter's publication

It was thought that the Letter was going to be ready for Easter, but in the end, it was signed on May 27, 2007 (Solemnity of Pentecost) and then published only at the end of June, the day after the Solemnity of Saints Peter and Paul.

Four days before the Letter's publication, John Tong and I received a copy—but there were problems. When using the computer, it is easy to make mistakes—and there were many. But more serious mistakes were in the Chinese translation. Some were not that serious, but one was very serious. Who were the translators? What a shame that a Letter addressed precisely to the people of China had so many errors in the Chinese translation.

There was also another problem: there was an attached document, author or authors unknown, which was some sort of presentation of the Letter. This attachment had useful material, but also some mistakes. One that was not very serious had the Letter say: "There are still illegitimate Bishops and this leaves the faithful confused";

in reality, in paragraph 8.11 the Letter says that the Holy See has legitimized many illegitimate Bishops, allowing them to remain in the CPCA, and this leaves the faithful confused. However, another point was much more serious. In the Letter, the Pope says that "some, in special situations, under pressure, have accepted to be illegitimately ordained", a rather benign expression, but the attached document says: "Some, caring for the good of the faithful and looking far into the future, have accepted to be illegitimately ordained." Now this is very different from what the Pope said. Of course, they are praising the illegitimate Bishops who care about the good of the faithful and had a forward-looking vision. If this is the case, does it mean that those who did not accept illegitimate ordination do not care about the good of the faithful? Are they shortsighted? This way of saying things is very unfair.

Not knowing how to react to these facts, I went to Taiwan to seek advice from Cardinal Shan. He was very wise. He told me: "You should make two distinct comments. One immediately after the publication of the Letter to praise it; the other, a few days later to point out the mistakes and the problems." I did as he told me.

Praising the Letter was the most natural thing to do because it is truly a masterpiece, balancing doctrinal clarity and deep understanding for all people.

But the problem remains. How can I publish a seriously flawed translation on *Kung Kao Po* and an attached document that does not respect the Pope's thinking? I was convinced that I had to give believers a faithful translation of the Pope's thoughts. So I worked for three days on a correct version, together with the expert of the Holy Spirit Study Centre in Hong Kong and a confrere of mine in Taiwan. I published it on *Kung Kao Po*, also in the form of a booklet.

Meeting with the Pope in July 2007

Providence provided me with an opportunity, one that was very special to me, of meeting the Pope. The permanent deacons of our diocese were making a pilgrimage to Rome, but the Pope was in Lorenzago di Cadore, not in Rome, for his summer break (in a villa owned by the diocese where the staff of the diocesan seminary usually spent their holidays).

The deacons were willing to go and see him there. But it was said that the Pope did not give an audience in such a period. His habit was to walk to the square at noon on Sunday to recite the Angelus with the faithful. I wrote to the local

Bishop. Since there really weren't any others to worry about, he replied that we were welcome. Upon hearing this, the Pope told the head of the Vatican gendarmerie: "Will Cardinal Zen be able to come here?" After reaching an agreement with the local police, the answer came: "The Cardinal needs only to come to Venice; he will be brought here by helicopter." I asked: "What about our deacons?" The answer: "As long as they arrive in Venice, our police will lead the way for them." That Sunday at noon we were not only able to see the Pope but went on the platform to kiss his hand and receive a rosary. I was so full of joy, ready to return to Venice, when I was told that the Pope had invited me to lunch. You should know that Pope Benedict did not often invite people to lunch, unlike John Paul II who often did. There were six of us: the Pope and his secretary; myself and the Patriarch of Venice; the local Bishop and Father Lombardi, director of the Holy See Press Office.

(Do you want to know the menu? Very simple. Some spaghetti [to avoid getting the Pope's white cassock dirty a napkin was put around his neck like they do with children]. Afraid that the main course might include beef, which does not agree with my diet too much, I ate a nice portion of spaghetti; but the second was a nice piece of pork [the Pope comes from Bavaria, where they usually eat pork]. At the end, the dessert was a good tiramisu, and a nice espresso.)

Reaction to the Letter within the Church in China

During lunch, the Holy Father told me that ten days before the publication of the Letter he had sent a copy to Beijing, as a gesture of courtesy so that they would know about it in time. From Beijing came instead a phone call, saying that they would not allow the publication of such a Letter. The Pope's personal secretary replied that the Pope did not intend to ask for permission; he only intended to let them see it beforehand. They argued insistently, and the answer they got was that the Letter was going to be published.

The strange thing was that on the day of the Letter's publication everyone, even in China, could find it on the Internet and copy it. On the second day, the Letter had disappeared from the Chinese Internet, but by then many already had a copy of it.

What was even stranger is that in China the authorities did not react forcefully in public, only in private. They forbade priests and the faithful to study the Letter together and, of course, to obey it.

Unfortunately, on July 22, the day we met the Pope, China's official community celebrated the fiftieth anniversary of the foundation of the CPCA, and almost all the Bishops and priests took part in the event. I think that, if there had been the "advance Letter", perhaps the government would not have dared to go ahead with this celebration, for fear of insufficient participation (the Chinese Communists will never take risks if they do not feel secure). The Bishops and priests were under great pressure, but an advance Letter from the Holy See could have achieved the miracle of uniting them and leading them to act courageously, thus changing the course of history. Unfortunately, they were able to celebrate "in all normalcy" the fiftieth anniversary of the CPCA.

In the meeting with the Pope, I also spoke about something else. In the "attached document", a commission is frequently mentioned. What kind of commission is it? The Pope said that it was only a commission that was responsible for the Letter's publication. I reminded the Holy Father that we had talked about a real commission, like the one that once existed for Russia. The Pope said: "Of course, I'll convene it." In September he announced the establishment of the commission, and in November the first plenary assembly was held.

Thus, Pope Benedict has done two great things for the Church in China: a Letter and a commission.

The overly tolerant attitude
of the Holy See

In 2006 and 2007 several things happened: illegitimate episcopal ordinations and the celebration of the fiftieth anniversary of the CPCA, especially after the publication of the Pope's Letter. The Holy See has not always reacted forcefully.

Many illegitimate Bishops have been legitimized. At the time of Cardinal Tomko, they proceeded very cautiously. They inquired whether there had been any really major pressure, if the person was decent, if he showed that he loved the Church, and so forth. But later, they proceeded with less care, as if by inertia, with the danger of creating an impression, as if to say, "Let yourself be ordained illegitimately anyway; sooner or later you will be legitimized." I often complained about this to the officials of the two dicasteries. I brought it to the attention of the Holy Father, but it seems that not even the Pope could do anything about it.

The three of us before the Pope

I made a bold request to the Pope: that of having a discussion in front of him between me and the two—that is, the Secretary of State and the Prefect of the CEP. I should not have made that request.

It might have embarrassed the Holy Father, but he accepted. The meeting took place the evening before the start of the works of the commission for the Church in China.

I had prepared the summary of what I was going to say and made a copy for them. There were two things. First thing, their strategy was wrong, all about compromise and surrender. Since the Church in China still had so many healthy forces, why commit suicide? Many Bishops, priests, and faithful are courageous. The officials of the Curia make them appear to be in error. The Curia has always tried to please the Chinese government.

Second thing, they didn't listen to us, who come from the front line. I have the direct experience of seven years of teaching in the official seminaries of the Church in China. The government treated me with great kindness, but I saw how they kept their Bishops, priests, and faithful as slaves. And things have not changed according to the information I receive almost every day from China. Why don't they listen to us?

The Holy Father obviously could not say who was right and who was wrong. He said: "Cardinal Zen has been frank in expressing his point of view. We shall take that into account, right?" And the two of them, to defend themselves, said: "But, Cardinal Zen, we obey the Holy Father. The last word is always that of the Holy Father." "I suppose it must always be like that," I said. "However, sometimes the most important is not the last word, but the one before last. And that is always yours, not ours." The discussion ended there.

Correcting the mistakes in the Chinese translation of the Pope's Letter

The next day, the commission held its first meeting. The Secretariat had prepared the so-called *ponenza*, a brick of a volume. I struggled to read it all. I found out that they were accusing me of arbitrarily changing the official translation. Speaking about that, I told the Holy Father: "I should accuse them and now they accuse me. They manipulated the translation. What point is there to have a discussion in the commission when only a third of the members understand Chinese? I accept that we discuss things, but with an appropriate and competent group. I have already sent out a corrected version with the disc to the people concerned, telling them that we have helped them to correct the translation. Discussing it now in the commission makes no sense." The Holy Father ended telling the Prefect of the CEP to fix the *ponenza*, putting aside this problem.

Thus, the translation was flawed. Our correction was not authorized. We had to do it to avoid having the faithful end up with a falsified version of the Pope's Letter. We withdrew our translation, but the problem was still there.

Fortunately, in the Holy See there was an official in charge of translating pontifical documents: Paolo Cardinal Sardi, who was Archbishop at the time. I turned to him and he said to me: "Surely mistakes must be corrected, but I cannot rely only on Your Eminence's word. Please, get the views of other competent people." So I asked two Bishops from Taiwan, Monsignor Joseph Wang and Monsignor Joseph Ti-kang; the rector of Taiwan's Catholic university, Father Li Chen; and Father Mark Fang Chih-jung, the most famous Chinese Bible scholar. They checked the ten errors I had noted. Archbishop Sardi asked the CEP to make the necessary corrections, which they refused to do. Thus, on his own authority, Sardi had the corrected version posted on the Vatican's website (Vatican.va). The corrected version appeared on the site on October 24, 2008, more than a year after the Letter's publication, after so many people had already read the wrong version.

Throughout this process, we could see the gap between the Pope's way of thinking and that of the people who were supposed to support it, and who instead distorted it. There was one particularly serious mistake, as we shall see. And it could have only been deliberate rather than an oversight. The faithful might be scandalized, but similar episodes are not unheard of in history. Still, they are astonishing.

Why did the Holy Father not speak out himself? Pope Benedict is a saint, a great theologian, but he has a weakness: he is too good, too humble, too tolerant.

Once upon a time he got the nickname "God's Rottweiler" because, as Prefect of the CDF, he had to defend the faith and sound the alarm when he saw mistakes, but he always did so gently, without discourtesy or rudeness.

Pope Benedict is the mildest-mannered person in the world; he does not like to use his authority to solve problems.

The Archbishop Primate of the Church of England is a close friend of Pope Benedict. Once, I met him and asked him, "What do you think about our Pope Benedict?" He gave an answer that seems quite appropriate: "He is very shy."

One day I, a sinner, dared to complain to the Pope and told him: "Holy Father, I can't take it anymore. You want me to help you with the Church in China, but I only have words; you have the authority and you are not helping me. Not even Bertone, who is my Salesian confrere, is helping me. What is going on?" He replied, "Sometimes one does not want to offend a person"!

3

DRAFT, SUGGESTIONS, AND FINAL TEXT, AND CORRECTIONS TO THE CHINESE TRANSLATION

Third Lecture
June 21, 2017

I did three things after the publication of the Letter of the Pope to the Church in China:

1. Compared my suggestions and the final text of the Letter.
2. Corrected the mistakes in the Chinese translation.
3. Noted the serious omission (mistake) in paragraph 7.8.

Comparison between the draft, my suggestions, and the final text of the Pope's Letter

I had presented four pages of suggestions. When I got hold of the final text of the Letter, I compared the two, and I was very happy to see that the Holy Father had agreed with almost all of my suggestions.

1.2 There were words that seemed to me excessively laudatory—for example, when in the initial greeting he applies to China the words of the Apostle Paul, who says, "Your good name has spread all over the world, all the Christians admire what you do" (see Col 1:6–8). I explained my thoughts by saying: "These words are good for some people, but not for all the members of the Church in China, especially after two illegitimate episcopal ordinations took place in April and May with the participation of many Bishops."

The Pope removed those words. Truly, after the defeats of that year, there was little ground for too much optimism.

4.3 Dialogue is not a simple thing. It is not easy to reach a good outcome for both parties. The draft said that "it takes time." I said, "Yes, but you have to explain why it takes time and how long it takes." The key point is having good will on both sides. If this is missing on one side, the deadlock can last for a long time, and perhaps we can never reach a good outcome.

Now it seemed that our negotiators were in a hurry to reach an outcome. But if the other side wants you to give in and you cannot do it, there will be no outcome. The success of dialogue does not depend on us alone, but on the other side as well. In that case, it takes the Lord to convert hearts. The Holy Father added in the Letter that it "presupposes the good will of both parties".

6.2   Toward the end of the paragraph, quoting the words of John Paul II, the draft said: "Even missionaries make mistakes, people in the Church make mistakes, because we all have our limits; there are also the circumstances of history, especially the political situation of the time." I said: "The Communists are very happy to hear that our missionaries followed the imperialists to invade our nation." If the Communists in China were successful, it was not through Marxism. Even in their fight against religion they did not use Marxism. Their success was due to their anti-imperialism. Therefore, acknowledging the mistakes of the missionaries plays into their hands. The words of John Paul II are true. There were imperialist elements also in the Church in China, but they are already relegated to the distant past. When the Communists took power, our missionaries were anything but imperialist. Bringing the conversation back to the remotest past plays into the hands of the Communists. The Pope understood my concern.

7.7 Toward the end of the paragraph the draft said: "There must be relations between our Church and the Government because we live in this political reality; consequently, it is good to have lines of communication." Given the context, this seems to imply that we must keep the CPCA, but this is not appropriate. The draft already said that the CPCA is not acceptable. In fact, the name of the association is already foul-smelling; whatever changes are made in its substance, the faithful will not accept it. If the name is changed but the substance is kept, people will not accept it either. The Holy Father removed the sentence.

7.8 This paragraph is particularly important. We shall talk about it later.

7.9 The draft included many moral questions. Yes, they were relevant but quite complicated. It said that we must avoid scandals, that we must nurture the conscience. It said that the most important thing is harmony and understanding and that we must avoid accusing one another. Finally, it said that if someone has no freedom, we cannot be too harsh in our criticism of their actions. All this seems right. However, if it recommends not to be too easily scandalized while recommending to nurture our conscience and judge good and evil, then how can one not criticize? What is more, harmony and understanding cannot come at the expense of the truth. The draft cites the First Letter to the Corinthians: "'Knowledge' puffs up, but love builds up" (8:1). While it is true that knowledge alone leads to pride, if one believes that love is so important and that, for it, one is allowed to neglect the truth, then we have a dangerous contraposition between knowledge and love. The Holy Father agreed with me.

8.2   The draft said: "They have so 'demeaned' the Petrine and episcopal office." In the discussion, some proposed the verb "diminish" or "damage" instead of the verb "demean", which seemed too strong to them. I, however, insisted that the word "demean" was just what we needed, because in my experience teaching in seminaries in China, I saw that government officials show no respect for our Bishops (in the official community); actually, they continuously humiliate them. The pope agreed.

Do you know how they bully the Bishops into taking part in illegitimate episcopal ordinations?

They go to them and order them: "Come with me!" Once at the hotel, someone immediately takes them into custody. They have to hand over their mobile phone and, in the morning, they come to dress them up in the vestments and take them physically into the church for the ordination. To say that they "demean" the episcopal ministry is proper.

As evidence that they demean the Petrine ministry, it is enough to remember the celebration of the fiftieth anniversary of the CPCA and later the fiftieth anniversary of the first illegitimate ordinations. They act as if the Pope does not exist.

· 8.9   The draft almost said that we must thank the Lord because now all the Bishops in China are Chinese. But let me say, "Is this something for which to congratulate ourselves? They are all Chinese because the missionaries have all been expelled. But we still have great need for missionaries." The Pope did not include the text.

8.11   Here the draft dealt with illegitimate Bishops. It was already a good text. It said that, given the circumstances of the time, quite a few Bishops were ordained illegitimately. Acknowledging afterward the mistake they made, they asked for the Pope's forgiveness. The latter, after an investigation and with the consent of the legitimate Bishops of the area, legitimized a number of them.

Accepting the suggestion of several participants in the meeting, the Pope made the final text even clearer. It said that it is unfortunate that some legitimated Bishops did not make public the fact of legitimation, leaving the faithful confused. Some didn't take any actions to show their new identity. Therefore, the Pope said that they must constantly take actions in accordance with their state of communion with the Successor of Peter.

If a Bishop, having asked for the Pope's forgiveness, is legitimized, but remains not only in the CPCA but continues to shout slogans in support of an "independent Church", here there is evidently a contradiction, not in what the Holy Father did, but in the conduct of these people. The Holy Father obviously expects them to make an effort to gain true freedom and truly unite with the Successor of Peter.

8.12   The draft spoke of "the existence of some non-legitimized Bishops", hoping that one day they too would be legitimized. The words are not wrong, because it is immediately followed by: "However, certain conditions must be fulfilled." Still, the fact remains that in some cases it is impossible to fulfill those conditions. Thus, hope in such cases is definitely unwarranted.

Currently, in the negotiations between the Holy See and the Chinese government it seems that an agreement already exists on the method of choosing Bishops. Now some claim that the Pope will have to recognize the seven illegitimate Bishops, including those who were excommunicated. Among the seven, two have failed to uphold the obligation of ecclesiastical celibacy. Thus, it will not be possible for them to meet the conditions for an eventual legitimation.

Correcting the mistakes in the Chinese translation

As noted in the preceding part, the Chinese version had translation mistakes. The CEP, which was responsible for the mistakes, refused to make the corrections. So Archbishop Paolo Sardi, who accepted my appeal that was corroborated by four competent experts, had the corrections published on the Vatican website. There were two kinds of mistakes: one was omissions; the other was a lack of precision, by providing inaccurate translations. One mistake was particularly serious, which we will consider separately in the following main section.

Omissions

1.1 In quoting the Letter to the Colossians, the translation, after the words "we have not ceased to pray for you", left out "asking that you may be filled with the knowledge of his will" (1:9). Now these are very important words, knowing God's will.

6.1 It speaks of harmony, quoting Vatican II's Dogmatic Constitution on the Church *Lumen gentium* (no. 1), which says that the Church is a sacrament of the "intimate union with God", then left out "and of the unity of the human race", which was precisely the point of the article.[1]

8.2 The words "by virtue of a vision of the Church" were left out. It is precisely this mistaken vision that is at the root of the debasement of the Petrine and episcopal ministries. They treat the Church as if she were like any organization that they can keep under control.

8.5 After the words "have offered" they failed to add "and continue to offer" (which immediately precedes "a shining testimony"); this testimony is still shining both in the underground

---

[1] The *Lumen gentium* quote is an internal quotation from John Paul II's *Novo millennio ineunte*, no. 42.

community and, often, in the official one. We have seen many shining testimonies of Bishops in very difficult situations so that, confronted with these testimonies, we feel so humble.

8.5 Toward the end of the paragraph, after talking about the preparation of priests, religious, and laity, the following words were missing: "and making the necessary resources available". They too are important.

Inaccurate translations

3.1 The text says that "in recent times, it [the people of China] has also moved decisively towards achieving significant goals of socio-economic progress". Here, the adjective "significant" does not mean "of deep meaning" as it is translated in Chinese, but simply means "considerable" (in Latin the adjective "maxima" was used).

3.2 Where it says that the "Church ... with discretion [*con discrezione*] offers her own contribution", *con discrezione* is translated as "cautiously", but here the meaning should be "humbly".

7.1 The Chinese translation of the phrase "entities that have been imposed as the principal

determinants" needed a rewrite, which was done
in the amended version. It was particularly
important that the word "imposed" be kept; in
the first Chinese translation, that was not clear.

7.7 "Cultual" was translated as "cultural",
rather than as "cultic". Clearly, this shows the
translator's incompetence.

8.0 In the subheading "The Chinese Episcopate
[*Episcopato*]", *Episcopato* may also mean "Bishop's
Office", but here the translation should have been
"the Bishops".

Serious mistake in 7.8

Was the serious mistake (omission) in 7.8 over
the issue of whether to emerge from the underground or not? (Oversight? Or instead a volun-
tary omission?)

"Indeed almost always"

We had already amended the draft of this paragraph during our discussion, but the final text
given by the Pope is even clearer. The question
was precisely whether one can come out of hiding and be part of the official community. The

Pope says that it would not be a problem per se because we have the right to work in the open. However, if in order to exercise this right they ask us to forsake the principles of our faith and the communion with the universal Church, then we cannot do it.

The reality is that the Chinese government does just that: "in not a few particular instances . . . indeed almost always". Now the parenthetical element "indeed almost always" disappeared in the Chinese translation. Such an omission makes a huge difference. If the government almost always imposes those conditions—membership in the CPCA, support for the threefold independence of the Chinese Church, support for episcopal ordinations without pontifical mandate—how can we give in?

Obviously, someone wanted to encourage them to come out of hiding. In fact, after the publication of the Pope's Letter, many did come out saying that this is what the Pope wanted and that there is no longer any justification for remaining underground. Now this is not true. The original text clearly includes an invitation to caution.

Some people mention certain exceptions as examples. Some examples go back many years. At the time, the situation was very different. There is also the example of Bishop Lucas Li, but his is a unique case: he was very strong in his faithfulness to the Church, and his clergy were very close to him. They managed to come out into the open without joining the CPCA.

What follows the omission in paragraph 7.8

After the publication of the Pope's Letter, I wrote to the Holy Father, pointing out the following.

If the government almost always imposes unacceptable conditions, the conclusion should be "don't even try". However, the Letter "leaves the decision to the individual Bishop". This means putting a huge burden on the Bishops' shoulders. The government will put pressure: the Pope says you can come out; why don't you do it? Priests will put pressure on the Bishop. Priests used to tell the faithful that it was a sin to receive the sacraments in the official community. Now the Pope is saying that the faithful have the right to receive valid sacraments. The faithful, even if their heart is in the underground community, feel pressured to use their right because it is always risky to receive the sacraments in the underground community. In that case, even priests will feel tempted to come out into the open because, to put it bluntly, they will lose many followers in the new situation.

Some Bishops did try to come out into the open but realized that the government almost always imposes unacceptable conditions. They end up finding themselves in a confused and uncertain situation.

The Baoding case

Behind the facts there is the Baoding case. The Pope had to leave the decision to the Bishops (which cannot be said to be wrong), because had he said not to act, he would have virtually disavowed what the CEP had already done with regard to the Diocese of Baoding. So let us clarify what happened in Baoding.

The Diocese of Baoding is one of the strongest underground dioceses in Hebei. By 2006, the Bishop of Baoding (Jacobus Su Zhi-Ming) and his Auxiliary (Francis An Shuxin) had already been in prison for more than ten years. The government told An Shuxin that he could come out, and that they would recognize him as Bishop. The condition he had to meet was to concelebrate with Su Chang Shan, the illegitimate Bishop of the same diocese. An Shuxin did as the government requested with the approval of the CEP.

Su Chang Shan, ordained in 2000, later repented and asked to be legitimized by the Pope. He was told that Baoding already had a Bishop and so he could not be legitimized. The Pope forgave him regarding his illegitimate ordination and told him to behave like a good priest. Su Chang Shan in fact did follow the Pope's order: since then he hasn't dressed as a Bishop anymore. Even when he concelebrated with Monsignor An Shuxin, the two viewed the Mass as a concelebration of two brothers in the priesthood. But the priests in the diocese were really astonished, wondering how come their Auxiliary Bishop, who bravely lived in prison for more than ten years, now came out and concelebrated with an illegitimate Bishop.

It should be said right away that the CEP made two errors in this case because it did not consult the experts in the matter. The first mistake was that An Shuxin was not the Ordinary Bishop. Upon receiving the government's request, he should have replied by asking for Monsignor Jacobus Su Zhi–Ming's release first; otherwise, he would have appeared to his people as usurping the office of his Bishop: Did Rome perchance depose Su? What did Su do in prison that was so bad? The second mistake was that everyone knows that Monsignor An Shuxin is a good man, brave even, but he is not well educated; he is simple, and the Holy See placed him in a very difficult situation, that of dealing with the Communist government.

The priests in Baoding turned to the Holy See for clarification to see if what Monsignor An Shuxin did was correct. They also addressed the same question to the Monsignor who represented the Holy See in Hong Kong. The latter replied that if Bishop An really concelebrated with the illegitimate Bishop, then he did wrong. The answer from Rome was instead for them not to judge anyone. For now, they did not have an answer for them, but would clarify things eventually.

If the people in Rome had explained the actual facts, perhaps they would have reassured the priests, but by failing to provide an answer, they left the priests at a complete loss.

The fact is that Monsignor An ended up joining the CPCA, saying that "I am doing so if this is not against Church doctrine." But what kind of reasoning is that! It's like saying: "I deny the Immaculate Conception of our Lady, if this is not against Church doctrine."

Distressed priests wrote several letters to Rome, but Rome continued to support Monsignor An; indeed, they promoted him to the role of Bishop Coadjutor, telling the priests to obey him. The promotion, for the time being, had no real effects, but it does shape the future succession. Was Monsignor An suitable to be an Ordinary Bishop?

The government took him to Shanghai and Xi'an, where the two Bishops are also recognized by Rome despite their membership in the CPCA, and told him: "See how well these two dioceses work." Returning to Baoding, Monsignor An told his priests: "Those two Bishops are recognized by the Pope and are well respected even in the Catholic world. What's the problem with membership in the CPCA? You are the ones who have problems."

But his reasoning doesn't make sense. The status of the two Bishops is only temporarily tolerated by the Holy See, which hopes for a change in the future. Monsignor An, instead, has the right status and now wants the wrong one. They are already inside, and the Holy See tolerates that they remain so. His case and theirs are very different.

There is reason to believe that some priests who had already joined the CPCA were trying to bring Bishop An into it. At some point, the government told him to accept his installation as Bishop (as Ordinary Bishop, as everyone understood it). This time the Holy See told him not to accept the installation, but he accepted it anyway and then tried to justify himself by saying that he did so hoping to reclaim Church properties.

In 2010, Monsignor An took part in an illegitimate episcopal ordination. At the end of that year, he took part in the Eighth Assembly of Chinese Catholic Representatives. What a pity! A hero of the faith, who had suffered for ten years in prison, is now walking with those of the CPCA and seems to have no pangs of conscience.

We had to describe this in detail to help people understand that, given this fact, the Pope could not tell everyone in the underground to remain where they are. It would be like disavowing the work of the CEP.

So, two factors unhappily settled the question of coming out of hiding: the manipulation of the translation of the Pope's Letter (7.8) and the precedent set by the action of the Roman Curia in the incident in Baoding; without this precedent, the discussion could have its logical conclusion: "Don't try!"

3.6: Special mention and meditation on Revelation 5:4

Let's go to the discussion of an earlier paragraph that was not in the draft or suggested by anyone during the meeting: 3.6. It comes from the pen and the heart of the great theologian and mystic Pope Benedict, from one of his earlier General Audiences.[2]

He invites us to meditate on Revelation 5:4. In the vision, Saint John sees a book with seven seals that no one can open; he is anxious and cries. It is the book of history, and John was experiencing the persecution of the primitive Church and

[2] The Pope was quoting from his August 23, 2006, General Audience, cited in *L'Osservatore Romano*, English ed., August 30, 2006, p. 3.

must have asked himself why. Don't we often ask the same question? Only the sacrificial Lamb can open the seals and give us the answer (see v. 5).

Pope Benedict often quotes Saint Augustine to help us understand the mystery of history. Saint Augustine lived at an awful time in history. Rome was on the decline, invaded by so-called barbarians. A mighty civilization fell into the hands of barbarians. In the book *City of God*, he invites us to take the long-term view. Why does the Lord allow so many bad things in history? On the one hand, to show how man can become evil if he does not obey God. But on the other hand, says Saint Augustine, the Lord shows that he knows how to conduct things in a superior way.

Disobeying God can lead to many extremes, like the totalitarian regimes of Nazism and Communism: thousands and thousands of people slaughtered (I recently read a few books describing what Hitler and Stalin did). Pope Benedict lived under Nazism, and his nation was split in two by Communism. If you can, go and visit the concentration camps. There was worse: entire populations starved to death! The man who rejects God becomes more horrible than beasts and causes tragedies that our minds almost refuse to believe.

In such tragedies, the Lord shows the goodness of some people, as on Calvary, when the Roman soldier was able to see the Son of God in the dying

Jesus (Mk 15:39). A convict, disfigured, dies, but the centurion sees superhuman goodness. The Good Thief also saw his Savior in Jesus. Jesus guaranteed his salvation. In tragedies the goodness and fortitude of so many people become manifest; there is the supreme witness of the martyrs!

The Pope says that before the Passion of Jesus we are more than justified to ask why. Yet, it is precisely here that we find the answer: the sacrificial Lamb! He who has not sinned becomes sin, taking upon himself all the filth caused by us sinners.

We worship the Lamb who takes away our sins and worship the mystery of God's mercy in the darkness of human history!

One thing I think is important for you to know is that Pope Benedict does not easily put his signature to things written by others. In the first days after he took office, a secretary in charge of placing documents on the table for signing and then collecting them after they were signed, found them unsigned because, as the Pope told him: "I have not yet finished reading them." In fact, he wanted to read everything before signing. He is keen on this. Hence, we ought to read his Letter with attention to every detail!

4

COMMISSION FOR THE CHURCH IN CHINA: A "COMPENDIUM" AND AN "AID"

Fourth Lecture
June 22, 2017

We have spoken at length about the process by which Pope Benedict's Letter to the Church in China was prepared. It was a somewhat complicated process. Obviously, the Holy Father was the author, but the CEP had already prepared a draft. Suggestions came from the participants of the meeting in early February 2007. Some circumstances made it impossible for the Holy Father to say everything he probably wanted to say. It was, in short, an exhausting process. There were mistakes in the Chinese translation as well, and then an attachment that could also lead into error.

This reminds me of the prophet Jeremiah. When the king heard the reading of the scroll that the prophet had written in God's name, he cut it into pieces with his little knife and threw them into the brazier (see Jer 36:20–32). It seems to me that this, to some extent, was also the fate of the Pope's Letter to the Church in China.

The commission for the Church in China

The Pope's Letter was a great gift. But Pope Benedict did another very important thing. He set up an impressive commission to deal with the affairs of the Church in China.

In the days of Cardinal Tomko, Cardinal Ratzinger took part in those "joint and enlarged" secret meetings. After his election as Pope, I asked the Holy Father about setting up a commission for the Church in China, like the one for the Church in Russia. He said that he was thinking about it. In fact, toward the end of 2007, together with his Secretary of State, he put the idea into practice.

Members

Who were the members in this commission? People from the Roman Curia and people "from the front line": all the officials in the Secretariat of

State and the CEP, together with some staff who took the minutes; experts from the CDF (Cardinal Levada was Prefect at the time) and in canon law (Cardinal Herranz, a Spaniard from Opus Dei); and the representative of the Holy See in Hong Kong. Then there was us, almost equal in number, from the front line, so to speak—that is, five Bishops from Taiwan, Hong Kong, and Macau, and several experts (more than ten) from religious congregations who had worked or still worked in China—overall, more than thirty people.

The Holy Father did not participate in the work of the commission, but he always came to greet us, chatting with us for half an hour at the end of our annual assembly.

Meetings

How many times did we meet, and how long did the meetings last? The commission's annual meeting lasted three days. There were also the meetings of the Standing Committee, which consisted of about ten people. At the beginning, the committee met three times a year for half a day. This was changed to a full one-day annual meeting.

Agenda

What did we talk about, and who set the agenda? Ostensibly, we could all make suggestions. But in fact, the agenda was set by people in the Curia. On several occasions, we made some critical remarks at the start of the meeting. The president of the commission who chaired the meeting, Cardinal Bertone, was able to adjust the agenda. However, we wasted time. We felt that the officials from the Curia were afraid we might raise controversial issues. They wanted us to leave the latter to them and talk instead of more harmless things, like training, which actually took away more time, so that there was not enough time to talk about controversial and more complicated things.

Deliberations

Were any decisions voted on? Almost never. It is true that the secretaries were very diligent and recorded the discussions almost verbatim. However, since there were no such decisions and since it was impossible for everyone to read the long minutes, it was hard to see any consensus emerge in the meetings. What was most regrettable was the fact that the only time a decision was put to a vote, it seems to us that it wasn't respected by the officials of the Curia.

At the special meeting of February 2007, we had already talked about Mr. Liu Bainian, the man responsible for the illegitimate episcopal ordinations of 2006. We had talked about excommunicating him, issuing and sending him a warning, but then everything was forgotten. When the commission met in 2007, we realized how dangerous it would be to collaborate with this man, because we would end up having to obey him. Many years ago, Belgian priest and China expert Father Jeroom Heyndrickx came up with the good idea of organizing seminars for the Bishops in China on the topic of diocesan administration. He planned to invite ten Bishops. Mr. Liu Bainian's permission was needed, though, and in his reply, Liu said that on our list, five were fine, but five were not; he would add the other five. What could we do? If we didn't accept his conditions, nothing would be done. When Father Heyndrickx consulted us, we ended up saying never mind and that we would accept his conditions. At least five would be the ones we want, hoping that this would do some good to the other five, who would have an opportunity to learn about the true Church in the world.

We saw no major drawbacks in having one or two seminars. However, in the long run we realized we were boosting Mr. Liu Bainian's authority in the eyes of both the government ("foreigners obey me") and the Bishops ("those who obey him will have the opportunity of traveling abroad").

We spent one half of the three days of the annual general meeting on this topic. So the issue was put to a vote (with the officials of the Curia exempted from voting), and the result was almost unanimous: to end the collaboration. But then? The Curia allowed this collaboration to continue as before!

Communiqués before and after the meeting

At the beginning, the meetings were totally secret. Eventually, since it was impossible to keep it secret, at least the dates of the meetings were communicated, withholding the names of participants and the topic of the meetings.

Later, pushed by the media, a statement would be released after the meeting saying nothing about the most sensitive items. Finally, it was thought that greater transparency could make the work of the commission more effective, since press releases were a means of sending messages to the Bishops in China.

The making of the "Compendium" and the "Aid"

At the beginning, a lot of the time was taken up discussing problems concerning the interpretation of the Pope's Letter, especially on the question of whether those from the underground community could or should come out into the open. We have already outlined the great discussion on the topic.

One answer to this can be found in the document called the "Compendium".[1]

The "Compendium"

A year after the publication of the Letter, during the meeting someone noted that it didn't seem to be widely known. Something had to be done to make it better known. Someone suggested inviting people to write on the topic. In the end, it was decided that a compendium would be drafted on behalf of the commission. The compendium had to be based on what was in the Letter. In other words, it would be a short version of the Letter.

I took the liberty of saying that such a compendium could be useful. After our long discussion, it could provide an opportunity to clarify things, especially on the particularly controversial point. After long and hard deliberation, the Holy Spirit Study Centre in Hong Kong, which had been commissioned to write the compendium, was allowed to propose some footnotes. There were seven in all. The second one was

---

[1] The "Compendium" can be found on the Vatican's website.

especially important because it highlighted the difference between *reconciliation*, which is at the level of minds, and *unification*, which instead concerns structures.

Father Heyndrickx and others insisted on unification right away, while the Pope spoke of reconciliation and said that unification is a long and hard road that will also require the government's good will.

After many years of separation between the two communities, we noted that the situation varied from place to place. In some cases, the two communities coexist peacefully. In others, relations are conflictual, and leave bitter feelings in the heart. With a policy of openness and greater opportunities to meet, reconciliation was an attainable goal. But where could we achieve true union? Should everyone be invited into the underground community? That is not possible. Push everyone into the official one? How could this be done when the latter is in an abnormal situation that is contrary to Church doctrine?

Thus, without delay, let us set off working hard for reconciliation, boosting mutual understanding. After all, everyone was a victim of a situation imposed from the outside that did not depend on them. If circumstances allowed, we might even meet over a cup of tea or even discuss pastoral problems of common interest.

An "Aid"

As we got ready to discuss the content of the "Compendium", the Secretaries of the Curia came along to say that they planned to submit another booklet as a way to make the Letter more widely known. At that point, I said that I too would prepare another booklet, one entitled "An Aid for Reading the Holy Father's Letter to the Church in China". When they took a look at my "Aid", they said they would drop their booklet, hoping perhaps that I too would drop mine. That's what I did. However, I also said that I would not publish it in the name of the committee but in mine.

Someone said that it would still carry the authority of a Cardinal. Monsignor Parolin asked me if it was not advisable to get the opinion of the Holy Father. How could I say no? After a few days, the answer came from the Secretary of State, who was not a member of the Standing Committee: the Holy Father said that those parts of the "Aid" that the committee has agreed on could be published in the diocesan weekly *Kung Kao Po*, but not the whole text. I was taken aback. The contents of the "Aid" were never discussed. There were no agreed parts, nor any nonagreed parts. What did they tell the Holy Father, asking for his opinion on my "Aid"? Obviously, the

Holy Father was misinformed (deceived?). Once this was cleared up with Cardinal Bertone, the publication of my "Aid" was allowed.

What is more, I can add that the Secretary who handed over my "Aid" to the Holy Father informed me that His Holiness kept it on his desk for a long time, which means that he read it carefully. In fact, after some time, when I had the opportunity, I asked Pope Benedict for his opinion. His answer was that the "Aid" was excellent.

My decision to prepare an aid for reading the Letter was also justified by what Pope Benedict wrote by way of clarification at the top of his Letter (2.2)—namely, that the latter does not claim "to deal with every detail of the complex matters well known to you".

I sincerely believe that the "Aid" can help understand some points not developed in the Pope's Letter.

Two regrettable events

Fiftieth anniversary celebration of the first illegitimate episcopal ordination

As noted, the government of China did not publicly slam the Pope's Letter, but did quite a few things against it, one of which was the celebration of the fiftieth anniversary of the founding of the CPCA, an event held almost immediately after the publication of the Pope's Letter. Since there was not that "advance Letter" to the Bishops, they were not ready to unite against such a celebration.

But now we were already at the end of 2008, more than a year after the Letter's publication!

Plans for this second celebration were not made public. Upon receiving information about such plans, I thought that taking part in such a celebration was a serious matter and that it would be like an act of defiance vis-à-vis the Pope's authority. I urgently traveled to Rome. The Holy Father asked the Chinese embassy in Italy for an explanation. The first answer was that they didn't have any information. Shortly thereafter, the answer became that they had been informed that preparations for the celebration were underway. Since everything was already in an advanced state, it would not be possible to cancel it. They would try to tone it down. Could anyone believe that?

The fact is that many Bishops and priests took part in the celebration of the fiftieth anniversary of the first illegitimate episcopal ordination, as if the Pope's Letter had never been written!

During the meeting with the Pope, with Cardinal Bertone present, I said: "It is all the fault of Ostpolitik. The willingness on the part of the Holy See to yield has encouraged the Chinese government to be more and more arrogant." At that point, Pope Benedict told Cardinal Bertone: "Do you remember, with respect to Ostpolitik, John Paul II said: 'Enough'?"

Eighth Assembly of Chinese Catholic Representatives

The Eighth Assembly of Chinese Catholic Representatives was set to take place. This assembly is the supreme authority of the official community and meets every five years. All the Bishops and the representatives of the priests, nuns, and faithful (in what proportion, who knows?) participate, some two hundred to three hundred people.

The assembly has the power to change the constitutions of both the CPCA and the Bishops' Conference. However, its main task is to elect the president and some vice presidents of the CPCA, as well as the president and some vice presidents of the Bishops' Conference (whose outcome is a foregone conclusion).

This is what they call the "democratic way" of governing the Church. It is the most explicit demonstration of the schismatic nature of the "official Church". After the Pope's Letter, how could such an assembly take place?

The commission in its statement said that participation in such a planned assembly was *not* permitted. We were not sure that such a ban would be effective, but the government, fearing that at least some Bishops might not dare participate anymore, would have postponed the celebration (the Communists are smart enough not to take risks).

Two or three Bishops came to Rome and told the Cardinal Prefect of the CEP: "Your Eminence, we are under enormous pressure. We do not know what they will do to us if we don't go to this assembly." The Cardinal Prefect answered: "We understand." Understanding is all right, but why not add some encouragement to be faithful to the Catholic Church despite the pressure? Those Bishops, upon their return to China, repeated the reassuring words of the Cardinal Prefect to their colleagues. Upon hearing this, the government felt secure enough to convene the assembly. Still, some hesitation remained, so they not only ordered everyone to participate, but literally "brought them" to the venue of the assembly.

(The participation of the Auxiliary Bishop of Shanghai, Monsignor Xing Wenzhi, astonished people. Probably, Bishop Jin Luxian, excused from participating because of age, told Xing that his absence would have been a calamity for his diocese. However, Xing was so uncooperative that the government later found a way to get rid of him.)

I cannot quite shake the conviction that the Ostpolitik of the officials of the Roman Curia undermined all the efforts displayed by the commission to help the Church in China.

5

CONTENT OF THE LETTER: CATHOLIC ECCLESIOLOGY

Fifth Lecture
June 24, 2017

Let's begin analyzing the content of the Pope's Letter to the Church in China.

Before the Letter's publication, a priest from inside of China wrote on UCAN that the whole problem between the Church and the government is a misunderstanding. For this reason, he hoped that Pope Benedict would put aside any big speculation and instead humbly and kindly seek an agreement.

But how can the Pope not be interested in doctrine? In fact, the Letter is valuable for its clear and profound doctrine.

The Holy Father did not change the order of the material in the draft. This order sometimes left something to be desired. In our analysis it is better to put a little more order—that is, without repetitions and dispersion. When His Eminence Paul Cardinal Shan of Taiwan presented the Pope's Letter, he summarized it in three parts. I thought that this division into three parts was a good idea, so all three parts are discussed in separate chapters: Catholic ecclesiology, the mission and structure of the Church (the theological problem), which is presented in this chapter; the situation of the Church in China—from division to reconciliation, and finally to unity (discussed in chapter 6); and the relationship between the Church and State regarding mutual respect and cooperation (discussed in chapter 7).

Catholic ecclesiology: The mission and structure of the Church

Mission of the Church

The Church's mission—that is, her why—is the only way we can understand her structure to fulfill this mission.

In paragraph 3.2, the Pope says that the Church is in the service of spiritual values like solidarity, justice, and peace. In 3.3, he says that in recent years China gave importance to economic and technological progress. Materialism and hedonism are the trends of modern society, and China is no exception. On the other hand, man, especially young people, feels the need for other values, especially spiritual values. By strengthening spiritual values, the Church precisely compensates for what is lacking in a society that strives for material progress.

Paragraph 3.5 says: "*Duc in altum*" (a reference to Lk 5:4, where Jesus tells Simon, "Put out into the deep"). This is an invitation to accept this challenge. It is quite appropriate to have the Church face the contradiction that exists in modern society and to acknowledge her part, that of spiritual values.

Paragraph 3.7 says that the Church's work is "to preach". Jesus tells the Apostles to go and preach all over the world. Preach what? The Kingdom of God. Jesus preached the Kingdom of God, and the Apostles preached Jesus, because in Jesus came the Kingdom of God. This Jesus, who died and rose, brought a "new Man". Jesus not only preached this "Man", but gave grace so that it could be a reality.

Paragraph 3.7 already starts to show how this mission requires its own structure. A fundamental condition is the union with the Successor of Peter and the universal Church.

The structure of the Church

Paragraph 5.2 says that what is true for the whole Church is true for the Church in China, in which the universal Church, which is the Church of Jesus, must exist. There is but one Church, but in every place, in every diocese, the Church exists. The four features of the Church are one, holy, catholic, and apostolic.

Paragraphs 5.3 and 5.5 mention that the foundation of unity is the same faith, the same Baptism. In his Letters, the Apostle Saint Paul repeats this truth many times.

Obviously, in everyday life, the Sacrament of the Eucharist and the Sacrament of Holy Orders are very important. Baptism brings us to the Eucharist, which nurtures our faith. And the sacramental life is guided by the Bishop. The Bishop follows the guidance of the Roman Pontiff. Apostolicity is very important.

Pope Benedict says a few times in the Letter that, thanks to God, the apostolic succession exists in the Church in China (5.3; 8.9). This is a crucial problem in the ecumenical discussion. We must look at history to see if the current Bishop really comes from the Apostles.

Paragraph 5.4 is almost the same as what was said above. Every local church is united in the person of its Bishop. But a local church, if it wants to be Catholic, must coexist with the College of Bishops and with the Pope at the helm. By *Collegium Episcoporum* we mean the body made up of all the Bishops in the Church. Therefore, the Pope and all the Bishops of the universal Church exist in the local church. For this reason, we remember the Pope and all the Bishops in the Eucharist. The Church is one, and her unity consists of the communion of all the Bishops with the Successor of Peter. Now, such communion must be visible and tangible. In a normal situation, the Eucharist is important because it is the support of the Mystical Body. It is in a Eucharist that the Bishop ordains priests. Baptism is also administered within the Sacrament of the Eucharist.

Again, the mission of the Church

We have insisted on preaching the spiritual values brought by Jesus. Here the emphasis is on the word "truth".

In paragraph 7.3 the Pope clearly states: "Truth and charity are the two supporting pillars of the life of the Christian community." Therefore, the Church of love is also the Church of truth. The Church, in order to be faithful to the Gospel, which Jesus consigned to the Apostles so that the children of God could unite in a family in peace, needs someone to protect the truth in this family. It is the truth that unites it and guarantees its development. This is precisely the duty of the Apostles: to ensure that the Church always lives in the truth given by Christ and that in this truth she always remains united. Love is supreme, but the foundation of true love lies in truth. It is precisely because we know who we are that we must love each other. For this reason, it is said that love gathers its strength from the truth and that the Apostles are truly the defenders and witnesses of this treasure of truth in the Church. To provide a service of love, one must lay the foundations on the truth.

Again, the structure of the Church

In paragraph 7.7 the Pope says that evangelization, catechesis, works of charity, liturgy and ritual activities, and finally pastoral choices are all things entrusted to the guidance of the Bishop with his priests.

(We have divided the whole content into three topics, but it is worth noting that paragraphs 7 and 8 already mention the inappropriateness of outside intervention in the life of the Church.)

Paragraphs 8.1 and 8.2 divide into three the various aforementioned roles of the Church. Here, instead of "evangelization and catechesis", the word "teaching" appears; instead of "liturgy and cultural activities", the reference is to "sanctifying"; and for the "works of charity and pastoral choices" the word "governing" is used.

Given the shortage of ecclesiastical personnel in recent times, in some places, by an official act of delegation, some roles mentioned above can also be entrusted to laypeople. For example, when a missionary is the head of a parish but does not yet command the local language, he can task some faithful to preach. Obviously, it is another thing when priests are not only replaced by lay believers but also by unbaptized people, atheists, or officials of the government. The latter cannot control or decide in matters that pertain to the life of the Church. Such abuses create a wrong image of the Church, debasing the Petrine and episcopal ministries (8.2). (As you can see, we are touching the third major topic again.)

Again, the mission of the Church

In 8.5 we are reminded that in modern society, with regard to the duty of Bishops to promote the new evangelization, a *major* problem emerges, that of relativism or subjectivism. Relativism suggests that there is no truth; there are only subjective points of view. This is dangerous. Therefore, the Pope advises the Bishops to train the clergy well with all means and resources at their disposal.

Then in 8.6, quoting John Paul II, comes a great assertion: For a "Bishop ... Christ is everything."[1] The Bishop must build up the family of God. Jesus is the head of our family. He is invisible, but the Bishop is visible.

In 8.7, quoting from one of his previous addresses, Pope Benedict clarifies once more the roles of the Church—using different terms, inferred this time from the Acts of the Apostles (2:42), that is, from the life of the primitive Church—the roles of "listening to the Apostles' teaching, the breaking of bread, prayer and fellowship."[2]

Again, the structure of the Church

Paragraph 8.8 reiterates that the "College of Bishops" means all the Bishops of the world, while a Bishops' Conference refers to the organization of some dioceses in local churches. (This is discussed in 8.13.) The concept of this conference perhaps still bears some examination because it does not come directly from the Holy Scriptures, but from the needs of the times during the development of the Church. Such conferences serve a practical

[1] Pope John Paul II, Homily for the Jubilee of Bishops (October 8, 2008), no. 4; cited in *AAS* 93 (2001): 27.
[2] Pope Benedict XVI, Address to New Bishops (September 21, 2006); cited in *AAS* 98 (2006): 696.

use. (Here too, of course, the connection with the third topic shows up right away since the Bishops' Conference, being local, has special relations with the local government; but these relations must not affect the life of faith and morals, which come under the purview of the Church.)

Some special remarks

We talked about the mission and the structure of the Church. The structure too comes from Jesus through the Apostles, but we have also said that faith is the foundation of unity. Faith is more fundamental than the sacraments.

Under normal circumstances, we must treasure the sacraments, because they are the most effective means of receiving God's grace. But if extraordinary circumstances should prevent the sacraments from being received, the Lord has a thousand ways to give his grace. Faith is more fundamental than the sacraments.

We referred to the special situation of today's society in which the role of the Church is to support spiritual values, including the *truth*. This was followed by the question of *relativism*.

When Pope John Paul II, who taught philosophy, became pastor of the whole Church, he wrote two encyclicals: *Veritatis splendor* (August 6, 1993), a very important and timely encyclical against relativism, and *Fides et ratio* (September 14, 1998), in which he thanks the Lord for the two paths through which we come to the truth: reason and the supplement of the faith.

Even Pope Benedict, for many years as Prefect of the CDF, wrote an encyclical whose main subject is social justice; but at the beginning of the encyclical he spoke at length about the title itself: *Caritas in veritate* (June 29, 2009). In the second paragraph of the Introduction, he says that "charity ... needs to be understood, confirmed and practised in the light of truth.... This is a matter of no small account today, in a social and cultural context which relativizes truth, often paying little heed to it and showing increasing reluctance to acknowledge its existence." In the third paragraph of the Introduction, he says: "Only in truth does charity shine forth.... Truth is the light that gives meaning and value to charity." And by truth he means reason as well as faith.

Pope Benedict often says that without the basis of truth, love becomes sentimentalism, and the word "love" is abused and can even be used to mean its opposite.

The expression "dictatorship of relativism" is his. Someone might say, "Can't the truth of faith be dictatorial?" At first glance, it may seem so; but

upon reflection, we see that this way of thinking is wrong. If there are only personal points
of view, who will be able to impose this point of
view? The rich and powerful, naturally. Con-
versely, if we recognize the existence of objective
truth, everyone is equal before it. Human rights
were born with man, not granted by the rich and
powerful. Defending this *objective truth*, guarding
that treasure of wisdom, is precisely the task of
the Church.

The Church's mission must be supported by the
structures intended by her Founder. But in
the community dominated by the government,
there is a structure that is, objectively, schismatic.
(In the private audience Pope Francis granted me
three years ago, when I told him this, His Holiness
whispered, "But of course".) It is the government
that runs the Church, with the result, as discussed
previously, that the Petrine and Episcopal ministries have been debased (8.2), splitting the Church
into two communities.

We are grateful for the precious things found in
the Pope's Letter to the Church in China, and
with the guidance of Cardinal Shan we have laid
this first point as foundation. Only from this can
we start to view the current situation and lead it
to the goal of complete unity.

6

CONTENT OF THE LETTER: SITUATION OF THE CHURCH IN CHINA

Sixth Lecture
June 26, 2017

In the previous section on ecclesiology, we stressed the importance of doctrine, and of truth. Let us remember that Pope Benedict, in his greeting at the beginning of the Letter to the Church in China, says that the purpose of the Letter was precisely that of knowing God's will, of knowing what Jesus expects from us.

On the basis of truth, we can now proceed to evaluate the present situation of the Church in China and its problems that need a solution—from division to reconciliation, and finally unity.

4.1 Pope Benedict says that he thanks the Lord "for the deeply-felt witness of faithfulness offered by the Chinese Catholic community in truly difficult circumstances." This testimony obviously means faithfulness to the nature of the Church and not endless yielding. The Pope sees "the urgent need ... to confirm the faith of Chinese Catholics and favour their unity with the means proper to the Church."

5.1, 5.6, 6.1.   In paragraph 5.1, the Pope says that, even if Chinese Catholics are but a "small flock", they still have a great mission: that of being "'the salt of the earth' (Mt 5:13)" and "'the light of the world' (Mt 5:14)". In paragraph 5.6, he states that the important thing is to rebuild "the harmonious hierarchical communion" and "to defend and to safeguard what belongs to the doctrine and the tradition of the Church." In paragraph 6.1, quoting John Paul II's *Novo millennio ineunte*, the Pope provides one word for this communion: "koinonia", which is "the very essence of the mystery of the Church".

The Second Vatican Council, at the very beginning of its most important document, the Dogmatic Constitution on the Church (*Lumen gentium*), says that the Church is a sacrament. (This caused great wonder in some faithful, as if they discovered one more sacrament than the other seven sacraments; in fact, the word "sacrament" is realized precisely in the Church because it is a visible means instituted by Jesus to signify and give invisible grace.) In what way is the Church a sacrament? The Church means and realizes the union of man with God and the union among men.

The topic is precisely the unity that is built with love. In paragraph 6.1, further referencing *Novo millennio ineunte*, Pope John Paul II has Saint Paul remind us in his "hymn to love" that without love, everything will be useless (cf. 1 Cor 13:2). The last sentence of 6.1, ending the quoted passage from *Novo millennio ineunte*, is: "Love is truly the 'heart' of the Church."

6.2, 6.3   Union is part of the Church's nature, but, unfortunately, at this time there are "tensions, divisions and recriminations" (6.2) within the Church in China. In 6.3, referencing his General Audience from April 5, 2006, Pope Benedict says that even the primitive Church went through such a trial, caused above all by the conflicts over the truths of the faith. The doctrine, for example, on the Most Holy Trinity is hard to understand. In trying to explain it, there have been violent discussions and unfortunately also heresies that have wrecked communion. The Pope says that the danger of losing the faith has always existed and consequently so does the loss of brotherly love. We must face this danger with a positive attitude and without fear.

6.4   There is no genuine communion "without arduous efforts at reconciliation" that entail the purification of memory, mutual forgiveness, and forgetting the wrongs endured—conscious that hardships come mainly from external pressures and that even those who make mistakes are themselves victims. We must keep the faith steadfast, but not focus on division. We must seek peace in love.

6.5, 6.6   While Pope Benedict was writing this Letter, the jubilee year of 2000 was still fresh in memory. Therefore, the entirety of paragraph 6.5 recalls a passage from a message by his predecessor given in preparation for the occasion of the Great Jubilee.[1] Saint John Paul II often spoke of reconciliation, saying that the Holy Scriptures entail the obligation regarding the forgiveness of debts, and an appeal to prosperous nations to cancel the debts of poor nations. Someone might say: "But debts must be paid!" Yes, true. The debtor has no right to demand to have his debt forgiven. But as the Pope put it, poor nations are already struggling to

---

[1] The quoted passage is from John Paul II, Message to the Catholic Community in China *Alla Vigilia* (December 8, 1999), no. 6; cited in *L'Osservatore Romano*, English ed., December 15, 1999, p. 5.

pay interest, and prosperous nations, by such an act of generosity, can allow these nations to begin finally to revive economically. Sure enough, many nations did heed the Pope's plea.

Thus, with respect to reconciliation one should not always start by asserting one's rights. God forgives us endless times. Pope John Paul II says: "My ardent desire is that you will respond to the interior promptings of the Holy Spirit by forgiving one another whatever needs to be forgiven, by drawing closer to one another, by accepting one another and by breaking down all barriers in order to overcome every possible cause of division." John Paul goes on to quote what Jesus says at the Last Supper: "By this all will know that you are my disciples, if you have love for one another" (Jn 13:35).

Therefore, unity is naturally the ultimate goal, but the road won't be easy. Paragraph 6.6 says: "This journey cannot be accomplished overnight"; it requires the good will of both parties. If the government created the situation, without a change on its part, no one knows when it will be possible to re-create unity.

6.7 This paragraph notes that this journey "is supported by the example and the prayer of so many 'witnesses of the faith' who have suffered and have forgiven". In the underground and official communities, there are many strong and exemplary Bishops, such as Monsignor Li Du'an of Xi'an, whom I remember very well. He was humble and patient, but also very upright and brave. He could build good relations with the government, but at the crucial moment could also say no. We must remember these examples and imitate them with patience and steadfastness.

The second note on page 8 of the "Compendium" mentions reconciliation: "spiritual reconciliation" must be differentiated from "a structural merger". Reconciliation is an urgent duty, in which we must immediately engage, not only with prayer, but also with actions, like having the two parties interact on pastoral matters. Only when true unity is achieved will there be only one Bishop for each diocese.

My "Aid" (page 19) also helps to understand reconciliation. The Pope tells the faithful of the underground community: You must appreciate in the persons of the brothers still under strict government control what can be appreciated because many of them have the courage to show their desire to be faithful to the Holy See. On the other hand, to those of the official community, the Pope says: You must appreciate the choice made by your brothers in the underground community. It is the right choice. It is only to free themselves from undue government control that they have gone underground, with all the burdens they must put up with.

For many years, the Church of Hong Kong has backed the Pope in his encouragement by acting as a bridge between the two communities. When we hear criticism from the official community against the underground community, we defend the latter by saying that their position is legitimate. Instead, when we hear the underground community criticize the official community as if they were all traitors to the Church, we say: "No! Not all of them! Because we know these brothers. We have lived together for a long time. Many of them are strong and brave, upholding the true faith while being in such an unfavorable structure."

This way of doing things has had excellent results. Therefore, we must not always try to please the interlocutor. Never sharpen divisions, but try to narrow the gap.

7.3, 7.4 Speaking of ecclesiology, we had said that, in the family of the Church, we need someone to guide us in discerning the truth. The Pope affirms this in paragraph 7.3 (by quoting his General Audience from April 5, 2006). This task was entrusted to the Apostles, especially Saint Peter. For this reason, we can say that the structure of the Church is not democratic. The truth is not maintained by pleasing people. We certainly must love everyone, even those with a different opinion from ours, both in the Church and in the persecuting government. But, says the Pope in paragraph 7.4, quoting Vatican II, "love and courtesy of this kind should not, of course, make us indifferent to truth and goodness."[2]

We note how Cardinal Shan correctly put ecclesiology at the top in order to guide all of our reflections.

7.8 Could the underground community join the official community? This is the great problem that we must face directly.

The Pope's Letter speaks clearly. In itself, there is not a problem, because we have the right to work in the open. But in actual fact, things are more complicated, because the government "almost always" imposes conditions that no believer can in good conscience accept, such as joining the CPCA, supporting an independent Church with episcopal ordinations without pontifical mandate, or concelebrating with illegitimate Bishops.

The Pope's conclusion is to leave the decision to the local Bishop, who must consult his priests and reflect upon all the consequences. But when

---

[2] Vatican II, Pastoral Constitution on the Church in the Modern World *Gaudium et spes* (December 7, 1965), no. 28.

the Bishop has made his choice, everyone must obey, however saddening it might be, because it is a question of maintaining unity.

We have mentioned that the translation of the Letter was manipulated. The text was corrected only a year later.

Starting with the notion that the underground condition is not normal, someone loudly called on all the members of the underground community to come out into the open. The Pope did not rule out the possibility of doing so, but neither did he encourage it. The text of the Letter clearly calls for great caution.

As previously stated, a note in the "Compendium" clarified the distinction between reconciliation and union. On page 31 of the "Aid" more direct questions are asked: Does the Pope's Letter forbid the Bishops of the underground community to try to come out? No, it doesn't. Does it encourage them to do so? No, it doesn't. The Pope asks them to use caution because there is not much hope in a positive result. As long as the government holds on to its current position and continues to impose unacceptable conditions, accepting such conditions is tantamount to surrender. Hence, it is very difficult to come out into the open.

The Pope left the decision to the Bishop because of precedents in the CEP, which, even before the Pope's Letter, had encouraged Auxiliary Bishop An of Baoding to come out into the open.

Now we sadly see how Bishop An, who had heroically suffered for many years in prison for his faith, has become a blind follower of the government.

On page 33 of my "Aid", I ask: If one firmly believes that a Bishop has erred by not respecting the conditions laid down by the Holy Father, what do priests or believers have to do? The Letter does not mention this situation, but in reality, this is what happened in Baoding. The Holy See told Monsignor An not to accept his installation as Ordinary Bishop of Baoding. Monsignor An accepted it and then also took part in illegitimate episcopal ordinations as well as the Eighth Assembly of Chinese Catholic Representatives. It seems that he lives within the CPCA without a bad conscience. I think that priests and believers who now abandon the Bishop, guided by their consciences, sorrowfully have no other choice.

In the current situation, going from underground to official condition is, for all intents and purposes, unlawful because the official condition is a schismatic structure.

What can be said about the possibility for official priests to go over to the underground community?

Is it possible? These priests are under government control! Will the government allow them to give themselves over to the underground Bishop?

Let us look at the case of the Diocese of Shijiazhuang (which for underground believers is called Zhengding).

Bishop Jiang Tao-ran of the official community in Shijiazhuang was not well respected by either the government or his priests, who questioned his suitability to be their leader. After his death, the official priests told the Bishop of the underground community, Monsignor Julius Jia Zhi Guo, that they were prepared to follow him. He accepted them, most likely encouraged by the Holy See, or someone led the Bishop to believe that this was the Pope's will. My question is, How can they be so optimistic? Are these priests now free from government control, just because of the death of the Bishop, who had no power over them when he was alive? Will the government really let them join the underground community? If it did, it is very likely that it was done with the aim of infiltrating the underground community.

Monsignor Julius Jia welcomed them for Chrism Mass on Holy Thursday. They came, but many underground believers stopped coming. (Are those new faces spies? Did the government send them to find out about what we are doing?)

These official priests eventually asked Bishop
Julius Jia for an assignment, which meant effec-
tively that we would have official priests working
in the churches of the underground community.
The faithful were afraid of that, but they couldn't
refuse them, because they had been sent by the
Bishop. After a while, the government inter-
vened, sending away the underground priest,
so that the official priest had for all intents and
purposes taken over that church. It was therefore
naïve to believe that unity was possible at this
point in time.

The principles are right, but problems persist.
Thus, avoiding criticism and trying to understand
each other are duties that are hard to implement.

8.3, 8.4, 8.5, 8.9   All of these paragraphs insist
on the importance for the Bishops to persevere
in defending the union with faithfulness to the
Successor of Peter.

We talked about the reconciliation between
the two communities. Now let us try to understand a little bit more the current situation of
the underground community and the official
community.

8.10   Let's see how the underground situation
originated. "Some of them, not wishing to be
subjected to undue control exercised over the life

of the Church, and eager to maintain total fidelity to the Successor of Peter and to Catholic doctrine, have felt themselves constrained to opt for clandestine consecration. The clandestine condition is not a normal feature of the Church's life [Some, citing this 'obiter dictum' out of context, turn it into a great thing, but the Pope's Letter goes on to say], and history shows that Pastors and faithful have recourse to it only amid suffering, in the desire to maintain the integrity of their faith and to resist interference from State agencies in matters pertaining intimately to the Church's life." The situation of the members of the underground community is burdensome. The government can always harass them.

Still, the government does not always suppress these communities. The situation varies from place to place. In some places, there are many underground believers who even have their own churches, even big ones. Many years ago, the underground community held large-scale public activities. For example, every year on May 24, approximately ten thousand people, including two or three Bishops and hundreds of priests, celebrated the feast day for Our Lady Help of Christians until one day a group of French reporters filmed the event and broadcast it on French TV. Since that day, this activity has been suppressed by the government.

In Hebei, Fujian, and Wenzhou, large numbers of the faithful and priests together with their Bishops can still do things that are obviously not possible in cities like Shanghai. Yet, many underground priests can celebrate Mass even in Shanghai with the participation of numerous faithful. The government certainly knows everything and tolerates it. They even allowed a big funeral for the underground Bishop Fan Zhongliang, concelebrated by all the underground priests plus some official ones, with some five thousand believers, including several Consuls General. Obviously, these priests face many restrictions. Their movements are limited. They are not always allowed to travel outside China. They cannot run the seminary in hiding.

It is almost possible to say that, in a sense, there is more freedom in the underground than in being "officially" out in the open. Why force those in the underground to give in?

8.11   Let's see how official communities came into being. Some pastors, "under the pressure of particular circumstances, have consented to receive episcopal ordination without the pontifical mandate". The Pope here writes in a way that shows understanding. We noted that in the so-called "Explanatory Remarks" to the Letter, this fact is not expressed in an acceptable way (see page 43 of the "Aid"). The "Explanatory Remarks" say that these Bishops did it because they care about the interests of the faithful and have set their eyes on the distant future, as if those who did not accept illegitimate ordination do not care about the interests of the faithful and are somehow short-sighted. For me, such talk is grossly unfair.

Popes understand these illegitimately ordained Bishops and then find reasons to legitimize them. In doing so, they avail themselves of the work of the CEP, especially under Cardinal Tomko. They knew that the circumstances were truly hard, and that disobeying the government meant death in prison; in their hearts, these Bishops wanted to be faithful to the Pope. The investigations show that they were honest and even capable people, and legitimation could facilitate the great union of the future. For all these reasons, Popes have legitimized many Bishops.

Some of the legitimized Bishops have shown themselves to be excellent and courageous pastors. Therefore, a clean-cut distinction between underground Bishops and those legitimized in the official community is not justified.

However, not all legitimized Bishops have behaved so well. The Holy Father complained that some, out of fear of the government, did not have the courage to let it be known that they had been legitimized. In which case, they ought to do it so, so as not to leave the faithful in confusion.

When Pope Benedict published the Letter in 2007, people wondered why, until then, legitimate Bishops were not asked to leave the CPCA immediately. Now, when the Letter says that they must make their legitimacy known, isn't this tantamount to asking them to leave the CPCA?

On page 45 of my "Aid" I say that not even after the publication of the Letter did the Pope ask for the immediate departure from the CPCA. However, he did recommend that the legitimized Bishops "provide unequivocal and increasing signs of full communion with the Successor of Peter". So if these Bishops continue to shout that they want an independent Church, they are contradicting themselves.

Even though he did not call on them to leave the CPCA right away, the Pope was not in self-contradiction. The Pope was hoping that they could do something to change things from inside the association. It is reasonable to think that the Pope wanted to say that the time was ripe; that they no longer had to have so much fear; that many Bishops had already been legitimized; and that the government knew that the illegitimate Bishops had a hard time being accepted by the people.

The existence of two communities certainly poses many problems. If the official Bishop is illegitimate, then the underground Bishop can excuse himself from dealing with him. But if the official Bishop is legitimate, what to do? Before legitimizing any illegal Bishops, Cardinal Tomko consulted underground Bishops. When he legitimized someone, the underground Bishop remained the Ordinary Bishop while the official one was legitimized as the Auxiliary Bishop, as was the case for Bishop Dong Guang-qing when he was legitimized in Wuhan. In Shanghai, Bishop Fan was the Ordinary. When Monsignor Jin Luxian asked to be legitimized, the Holy See was able to legitimize him only as a Coadjutor Bishop. Later, the Holy See appointed Xing Wenzhi as an Auxiliary Bishop.

There is a lot of confusion nowadays. We hear: "The official Bishop is legitimate. Everyone, follow him!" Many times, when old underground Bishops die, no one is appointed to succeed them; thus, underground communities have only an episcopal delegate. It is hard to run a diocese with only a delegate.

When the Pontifical Commission for the Church in China was first set up, there was an expert in canon law, a Spaniard, Julián Cardinal Herranz Casado. He was very competent (much more than those who succeeded him), and he gave a lot of good advice. He used to say: "How can a diocese, even if it had a legitimate official

Bishop, adequately take care of the faithful of the underground community without an underground Bishop?" In fact, at the beginning, there were Bishops for both communities. This expert used to say: "The Holy See can continue to ordain Bishops for the underground community. If a diocese did not have an underground Bishop and now the official one was legitimate, the Holy See can still appoint an Auxiliary Bishop for the underground community."

In several cases, the underground community now only has an episcopal delegate. An episcopal delegate is not a Bishop. An underground Bishop in a neighboring diocese can, with the permission of the Holy See, take care of such an underground community. If there is a legitimate official Bishop in that diocese, the neighboring underground Bishop must notify him of that. But sometimes the legitimate official Bishop unreasonably demands that the underground community come under his purview, and his alone. Since he is under government control, he is not free, so why compel the underground community to submit to this lack of freedom?

10.4, 10.5, 10.6 These paragraphs discuss the problem of *communicatio in sacris*. Recall the discussion of the eight points in chapter 1 above, where the fifth point said that the clergy of the two communities should not concelebrate. Later it was said that before the concelebration they must recite the Credo together. Then this too was dropped. Now, certain ways of doing things are really a source of doubts. How can one concelebrate with an official Bishop who, at every occasion, shouts out loud his support for an independent Church (on this, read pp. 55–58 of my "Aid")?

Regarding receiving the sacraments, it is obvious that one should preferably go to good legitimate Bishops and priests. For the Holy See, official priestly ordinations are valid, and thus the sacraments administered by these priests are valid. Even illegitimate Bishops administer valid sacraments.

There is the great principle that the faithful have the right to receive valid sacraments. Therefore, if it is dangerous or even cumbersome to receive valid and legitimate sacraments, they can avail themselves of this right. But while it is said that it is a right, nowhere does it say that it is a duty. Thus, if a believer thinks he can keep his faith while temporarily not receiving the sacraments, especially if he suspects that a priest lacks true faith in the doctrine of the Catholic Church and perhaps intends to force the faithful to enter the CPCA, then he can put aside the right to receive valid sacraments.

In the Church there is another principle that says: "God's grace is not bound by the sacraments."

God has a thousand ways to bestow his grace. But if one feels so strongly about receiving the sacraments, he should do it cautiously to avoid the aforementioned dangers.

8.12   The Pope says that there are other illegitimate Bishops who are not yet legitimized. Hopefully, once the necessary conditions are met, they too can be legitimized. However, we have to say, if such conditions cannot be met, there is no hope that the Pope's wish can be satisfied.

8.14   The Pope says that the Bishops' Conference of the official community is not legitimate, because it includes illegitimate Bishops, and legitimate underground Bishops "are not part of it". (These tried to join in a conference despite contrary advice from the Holy See. In fact, the whole thing turned out to be simply impossible. At the first meeting, only eleven showed up, even fewer for the second; meanwhile, the list with the names of all underground Bishops ended up in the hands of the government.)

The Assembly of Chinese Catholic Representatives stands above the CPCA and the Bishops' Conference.

Finally, outside of these structures, there is one person, Mr. Liu Bainian. It is widely believed that he is a member of the Communist Party of

China. He has been the de facto leader of the official community from the start. Although he is now thought to have retired and is only the association's honorary president, he still works hard. He personifies the abnormality of the official community throughout all these years.

9.1–4 These paragraphs discuss the appointment of Bishops, which is certainly a fundamental problem. Pope Benedict says: "On the one hand, it is understandable that governmental authorities are attentive to the choice of those who will carry out the important role of leading and shepherding the local Catholic communities, given the social implications which—in China as in the rest of the world—this function has in the civil sphere as well as the spiritual. On the other hand, the Holy See follows the appointment of Bishops with special care since this touches the very heart of the life of the Church.... For this reason the Code of Canon Law (cf. c. 1382) lays down grave sanctions both for the Bishop who freely confers episcopal ordination without an apostolic mandate and for the one who receives it" (9.1).

Pope Benedict rightly says that after all the most important thing is choosing the right people. In the absence of an agreement, the Holy See has tried to strike a compromise to ensure adequate suitability, even if at times it gives in to the aggressive demands of the government.

The method the government applies starts with a democratic election. The election has its problems, but one in particular is, in the case of a small diocese, how to find suitable people. Pope Benedict says that we must find them in neighboring dioceses (9.4). This is feasible within the traditional method of the Church because the responsibility of the Pope's representative is to start the consultation. But in the election, which takes place only at the diocesan level, ensuring the suitability of the candidate cannot be taken for granted.

Reconciliation is the most important issue today. Only after a long journey can we hope to reach unity. If the government does not recognize the rights of the Church, where will unity be achieved? For the official community, it is simply impossible to join the underground community. For the underground community, joining the official communiy is unlawful since the latter is under the absolute control of an atheist government.

7

CONTENT OF THE LETTER: RELATIONSHIP BETWEEN CHURCH AND STATE

Seventh Lecture
June 27, 2017

Having settled the ecclesiological foundation, clarified the current situation of the Church in China, and the direction it must take, now let us see what we can hope from Communism, this political, totalitarian power. Despite the hardships, we must hope. So here is the third topic: relationship between Church and State—mutual respect and sincere collaboration.

Paragraphs 4.2 and 4.3 say that we hope in a relationship of dialogue and collaboration, but we also know that this requires time and good will. If the latter is missing, there will never be a conclusion, because while we can accept certain compromises, there is a bottom line.

Paragraph 4.4 says that certain misunderstandings must be eliminated. However, reality is more than just a few simple misunderstandings. It is about steadfast positions. If a misunderstanding has to be eliminated, it is the idea that we are seeking privileges.

The same paragraph, citing Pope John Paul II, says that we hope to respect each other so as to work together on behalf of the Chinese faithful and the whole Chinese people.[1] We value stability and social harmony, because they are the bases of true progress. We are convinced that religious freedom will in no way prevent society's progress.

Paragraphs 4.5 and 4.6 quote from *Gaudium et spes*, whose article 76 says, precisely, in paragraph 4.5, that both Church and the State are "at the service of the personal and social vocation of the same individuals, though under different titles". We hold firm to this principle. But if the government wants to dominate everything, then this is not acceptable. Many governments understand that the Church must be independent, because there are spheres in life, like religion, that

---

[1] John Paul II, Message to the Participants of the International Convention "Matteo Ricci: For a Dialogue between China and the West" (October 24, 2001), no. 4; cited in *L'Osservatore Romano*, English ed., October 31, 2001, p. 3.

must not be under the dominion of the government. They might also have relations with the government, since both work in society and there is a need for them to collaborate in accordance with each other's jurisdiction.

In paragraph 4.6, another cited document is the encyclical *Deus caritas est* (God Is Love) by Pope Benedict himself. When the Letter was being drafted, this encyclical did not yet exist, but the quote precisely clarifies the question: "The Church cannot and must not take upon herself the political battle to bring about the most just society possible." For this reason, she does not establish political parties. That is not her task. This is the right meaning of what is called the "separation of politics and religion". But the second part of the quote follows: "[The Church] cannot and must not remain on the sidelines in the fight for justice", but must reawaken the spiritual forces because the pursuit of justice requires a spirit of sacrifice.[2] The word "politics" has two meanings: a narrow one—that is, party activity; and broad one—namely, interest in the affairs of society. The Church knows that it can contribute to society, especially with this supplement of spiritual energy.

---

[2] Pope Benedict XVI, encyclical letter *Deus caritas est* (December 25, 2005), no. 28; cited in *AAS* 98 (2006): 240.

Paragraph 4.7 says: "The solution to existing problems cannot be pursued via an ongoing conflict with the legitimate civil authorities," but there is also the other half of the quote: "at the same time, though, compliance with those authorities is not acceptable when they interfere unduly in matters regarding the faith and discipline of the Church."

Unfortunately, some people heed only the first half of these quotes and overlook the second half.

Let's jump to paragraph 7.1, which is very clear and important. It says: "The aforementioned painful situation of serious differences (cf. section 6 above), involving the lay faithful and their Pastors, highlights among the various causes the significant part played by entities that have been imposed as the principal determinants of the life of the Catholic community." This shows that the conflict between the official and underground communities did not arise from within the Church. It stems from the different reaction to the pressure of the government that wants to run the Church. So much so that they are in charge of the Church and are now not even trying to disguise that fact. There are pictures to prove it. When, for example, they say that the Bishops' Conference disqualified Bishop Thaddeus Ma of Shanghai, they show the picture of the conference session with Mr. Wang Zuo'an, director of the State Administration for Religious Affairs (SARA) at the seat of the president, with Bishop Ma Yinglin and Bishop Fang Xing-yao on his right and left, their heads lowered listening to his instructions. There is also another picture, a group picture, after an episcopal ordination. With Bishops and government officials seated interspersed, it seems to us so ridiculous, but for them it's normal.

The Church trains her seminarians. All over the world, the management of seminaries includes Bishops and priests, with some faithful. In China, seminaries are regional, and half of the members of management are Bishops from the dioceses from which the seminarians come and the other half are government officials. (Their annual meetings are a pretext for a tourist trip at the expense of the Church.)

With respect to the principles that govern the Church's conduct vis-à-vis the government, paragraph 7.2 cites the example of Jesus, who refused to be a political Messiah and asserted that he came to serve and offer his life (Mk 10:45).

Two other references are pertinent: Matthew 12:20, in which, quoting the prophet Isaiah (Is: 42:3), the Evangelist describes the meekness of Jesus, "who 'will not break a bruised reed or quench a smouldering wick'". He does not use force to crush the other, but is tolerant, waiting for conversion.

The other reference is the famous saying of Jesus: "Render therefore to Caesar the things that are Caesar's and to God, the things that are God's" (Mt 22:21). It should be noted, however, that in the last part, the two sides are not adequately differentiated, because, after all, what belongs to Caesar ultimately is God's, to whom everything belongs.

Paragraphs 7.3 and 7.4 are about the truth. We have already mentioned the truth elsewhere when we said that we must also love people who have different ideas from ours, but this "love and courtesy of this kind should not, of course, make us indifferent to truth and goodness" (7.4, quoting *Gaudium et spes*, no. 28). We hold fast to the truth, not because we love conflict, but because we cannot betray the truth, and hope that the government will accept it.

Paragraphs 7.5 and 7.6 also speak about the truth. Paragraph 7.5 says: "The claim of some entities, desired by the State and extraneous to the structure of the Church, to place themselves above the Bishops and to guide the life of the ecclesial community, does not correspond to Catholic doctrine." The Church is apostolic and must be led by the successors of the Apostles, the Bishops.

Later it goes on to say that, since the purpose of these entities is democratically to manage an independent Church (see the Constitution of the CPCA), this is not compatible with the Church's doctrine.

Paragraph 7.7 reiterates that, when the Church performs her proper tasks, she must not be subject to outside interference.

In paragraph 7.8, the Pope says that in principle no objection should be made to coming out of hiding and seeking government recognition. Unfortunately, in practice, the government almost always demands something that goes against our Catholic conscience.

Let's see the example of one case in Zhengding (Shijiazhuang).

A highly qualified priest from the Diocese of Zhengding was in a hurry to negotiate with the government his "coming out" while his Bishop was still in prison. The government promised him that on the certificate that he had to sign, the words "Independent Church" would be removed. The priest did not trust such a promise and did not show up to sign the agreement. Other priests, however, did and later complained when they saw that the words in question had not been removed. The officer said that they would delete them later. Suddenly they felt embarrassed that they had signed the certificate in such a situation.

Right afterward, the door of the room opened. In the next room there was a large number of people who came out to compliment the priests and offer them gifts. They had been tricked by the government.

Having given in once, they lost their dignity, and it will be hard not to give in again. The case of poor Bishop An of Baoding is one such example.

Paragraph 8.2, mentioned already, says that the Bishops "have encountered difficulties, since persons who are not 'ordained', and sometimes not even baptized, control and make decisions concerning important ecclesial questions, including the appointment of Bishops, in the name of various State agencies", causing "a demeaning of the Petrine and episcopal ministries by virtue of a [wrong] vision of the Church"; that is, the Church, objectively, has become de facto schismatic.

Let's examine more closely the means and agencies that the government uses to dominate the Church.

The Bishops' Conference

8.13   The term "Bishops' Conference" is distinct from that of the "College of Bishops", the latter being the group of all the Bishops of the world, while the conference refers to the group of Bishops of an area, especially a nation.

Since the conference is local, it also has a special relationship with the local civil government. This relationship, which should be normal, must respect the independence of the Church from the civil authority as regards to the faith and the life of faith (*Fides et mores*).

Pope Benedict said in his Letter that the Bishops' Conference in China is not legitimate, because it includes illegitimate Bishops and excludes legitimate Bishops from the underground community (8.14). In fact, the Bishops' Conference of the official community only has a name. It does not meet to address freely issues that pertain to the Church but only to receive orders from the government.

When I taught at the seminary in Xi'an, Bishop Li Du'an was one of the vice presidents of that conference. One day I asked him when the next meeting would be. He started laughing and said, "Dear Father Zen, do you think we have meetings? No, even when we just talk among ourselves they come to ask what we are talking about; we're summoned only to receive instructions."

Thus, the conference only has the name. The one body that does operate is what they call "an association and a conference"—that is, the CPCA and the Bishops' Conference, jointly. Mr. Wang Zuo'an, director of the Religious Office, chairs the meetings; the president of the CPCA and that of the Bishops' Conference sit beside him. The vice presidents of both bodies are trusted people who ensure that everyone present at the meeting obeys the government.

The Assembly of Chinese Catholic Representatives

As previously discussed in chapter 4, the CPCA and the Bishops' Conference are subordinate to the Assembly of Chinese Catholic Representatives, an assembly that is the supreme authority of the Church under the control of the government (the Pope's Letter does not mention this entity).

Recall that the Assembly of Chinese Catholic Representatives consists of all the Bishops and the representatives of priests, nuns, and the faithful, between two hundred and three hundred people. The Bishops, about seventy, have an individual vote like the other representatives. They can revise the statutes of the association and the conference. But its most important and practical role is to elect the top officials of the Church—that is, two presidents and a number of vice presidents. However, these elections are all preordained. In fact, the candidates sit at the table of the presidency from the beginning of the meeting. Is this what they call a democratic election? Although those elected are almost all Bishops, they count for nothing; they are puppets, led by the government. And who chairs this assembly? Until the Eighth Assembly (2010), it was Mr. Liu Bainian.

Mr. Liu Bainian

Here we must say something more about Mr. Liu Bainian. He is the main collaborator of the government since the CPCA was founded. During the years I taught at seminaries in China, I was able to observe his great authority. For example, when they treated me to a banquet with the presence of some Bishops and some government officials, we were the only two who spoke. But when he went away for a moment, everyone became talkative.

Bishop Fu Tieshan had invited me to teach in his diocesan seminary. When he met me, Bishop Zong Huaide, who was the rector of the national seminary, invited me to teach there too. I went there willingly. When I arrived, I saw that it was a seminary under the total control of Mr. Liu

Bainian. Bishop Zong Huaide was also president of both the CPCA and the Bishops' Conference, and thus the supreme authority in the official Church. But he could not make any direct international phone calls from his own office; for this, he had to go to Mr. Liu Bainian's apartment. How humiliating!

Mr. Liu Bainian was in charge of everything, even my meals (nothing to complain about there, though).

When traveling abroad with some Bishops, he is always the group leader, the one who speaks. Once a foreign host said: "There are some Bishops here. Can they talk?" He then pointed to Bishop Fang Xing-yao and said: "You talk." The latter became quite nervous, and as he was talking he always looked over at Mr. Liu Bainian. At the end he asked: "I didn't make mistakes, did I?" But the foreigners knew Chinese. How disgraceful for the Bishop.

In April–May 2006, two illegitimate episcopal ordinations took place. Mr. Liu Bainian tried to be inconspicuous, but many saw that he was in charge of everything. That's why, at the February 2007 meeting (discussed at the beginning of chapter 2), we proposed that a warning be sent to him, but the Holy See did nothing.

In the commission for the Church in China, the only vote we took was to say that one had to avoid cooperating with this man. But the Holy See allowed Father Heyndrickx to continue working with him.

As we have said, during the assembly the nominees sit at the table of the presidency from the start of the sessions. At the Eighth Assembly (2010), the government asked Liu Bainian to retire and appointed him as honorary president.

In the discussion groups (which have no authority), someone asked whether Mr. Liu Bainian should come back to work. One of the candidates for the post of vice president of the CPCA dared to say, "No! What does he want to do? Our young Bishops know very well what to do." When Mr. Liu Bainian heard about it, he confronted the Bishop: "In what way have I offended you? Why don't you want me to go back to work?" In the following session, the Bishop was no longer sitting at the presidential table. It is clear that Mr. Liu Bainian had the power to promote or dismiss anyone.

We have reason to believe that he is a member of the Communist Party. There was a Franciscan Father, a professor of Sacred Scripture at the seminary in Hong Kong, who taught at the national seminary in Beijing. He befriended Liu Bainian and placed himself at his service as a professor; and, as a German, he could also write letters on Liu's behalf to his benefactors in

Germany. After he finished teaching, he took his leave from Liu Bainian, telling him, "I am now going to Xi'an." Liu Bainian replied saying, "No one can teach in Xi'an." In 2000, Bishop Li Du'an disobeyed Beijing twice: he did not take part in an illegitimate ordination of Bishops and was not present at the signing of the protest Letter against the Pope's canonization of martyrs. The punishment that was imposed on him was precisely that no teacher from abroad could teach anymore in his seminary. The Franciscan Father said, "If you do not let me teach in Xi'an, I won't come to Beijing either." So Liu Bainian gave him a letter. When the German introduced himself to the authorities in Xi'an and was told that he could not teach in that seminary, he took out the letter. Upon reading the letter, the official immediately said yes. Liu Bainian must be a high-ranking party official.

The Ninth Assembly of Chinese Catholic Representatives

Let's get back to the Assembly of Chinese Catholic Representatives, which is the most explicit expression of the schismatic nature of that Church. In its statement, the commission for the Church in China told Chinese Bishops not to attend the Eighth Assembly (2010). Unfortunately, the Prefect of the CEP told some Chinese Bishops that they understood, and almost all took part in that assembly.

Shortly before the Ninth Assembly (2016) was about to take place, the spokesman of the Holy See said: "We know what this assembly is and we reserve the right to express a view on it with proven facts." This meant that people could attend the assembly. In the Eighth Assembly, although the government felt sure that the assembly could be held, it still had some fear that a few Bishops might heed the Roman commission. For this reason, it not only ordered everyone to go, but actually brought all of them to the assembly. On this occasion, they no longer felt the need to be cautious since Rome had given the Bishops permission to participate.

How could the Holy See send such a message? Was the commission perhaps wrong seven years ago [2010]? What does wait for "proven facts" mean? Don't they know how the assembly works? Are they waiting for a miraculous change? In fact, from start to end, they shouted that they wanted an independent Church. The Vatican spokesman had promised to talk about it after the events. We are still waiting for him to do so. If he is sincere, he will have to acknowledge that the government runs the Church in China.

Appointment of Bishops

Paragraph 9 deals with the important topic of appointing Bishops. The Pope's Letter is very balanced. On the one hand, he understands that the government is very interested in this since the Bishop is a public figure who influences society. On the other hand, he is aware that such appointments are of fundamental importance to the life of the Church. The Pope has tried to explain that his authority is spiritual and religious, not political; exercising such authority does not interfere with the government of the state. He also mentions that international conventions recognize that religions have the right to choose their leaders. In fact, large international corporations also have the right to appoint their local directors; so the Chinese government too must view as normal that Rome appoints its Bishops, a fact that is accepted by many nations in the world. Obviously, the Pope has not shut any doors and is willing to negotiate. He has said that, given the recent history of our relations, we accept to have an agreement with the government on such appointments.

In recent years, there has not been any written agreement but, in fact, there is an unwritten mutual understanding. The Holy See, once informed of the need for Bishops in certain dioceses, approves the names of candidates for this office. The names are not necessarily at the top of its list of candidates, but they are, however, acceptable to the Holy See for this office because they could hopefully also be acceptable to the Chinese government, even if they are not on top of their list. The names are approved, but no real appointment is made; the approval is secret but is leaked somehow to the Chinese side. The government sometimes accepts these names and so holds elections, and the Holy See then adds its seal of approval.

Sometimes the government insists on their names and the Holy See gives in to its insistence.

In 2010, nine Bishops were ordained with dual approval. Someone said: "Look! How beautiful!" and thought that Beijing accepted the Bishops appointed by Rome. I wondered, Is this true? I think Rome wanted some, while others were favored by Beijing. So who gained the most?

There was one name that Rome said it would never, *not ever* approve because of clear evidence of his unsuitability. Then he was approved (someone mockingly noted that "not ever" did not last long). What happened? Rome sent someone, a notoriously "good" guy, to carry out a new investigation, and he went to ask the person concerned if he had ever been part of any wrongdoing. The accused person responded no; the investigator reported it to Rome and Rome *was satisfied.*

Sometimes the Holy See does not feel right about approving, and so illegitimate ordinations take place. This was the case for the tenth ordination of the year 2010. These facts hurt the Church, but it is our impression that they are not even a great success for the government, because they must realize that the people do not willingly follow illegitimate Bishops or, worse, excommunicated ones.

Neither side likes to talk about this compromise in public. Perhaps they don't see it as very glorious, but it could have solved some situations albeit without any guarantee.

Many people view this kind of doing things as yielding too much on the part of the Holy See. The Holy See justifies this by saying that this is to avoid a possible schism, noting that if many Bishops are ordained illegitimately, the Church becomes schismatic. However, is allowing unsuitable people to become Bishops better than a schism? The Bishops who know they obtained this honor and authority, only thanks to the insistence of the government, will not feel any gratitude toward Rome and will not work for the true interest of the Church. A large number of these Bishops will form a schismatic Church with the blessing of Rome. Is it not better to let the world know that it is a schismatic Church? Besides, we believe that people want to become part of the true Catholic Church, so that as they see more and more opportunists in the government-run Church, they will abandon it. Historically, schismatic Churches have succeeded because they had some actual basis like differences in culture and tradition. A schismatic Church based only on the arrogance of a government will not last—and will fall with the fall of that government.

Some will say that historically emperors had the power to appoint Bishops. Yes, but they were Catholic emperors who favored the Church, and still problems developed. Fortunately, that way of doing things is now history.

In any event, having good shepherds is too important for the life of the Church. How can we deliver the flock into the mouth of rapacious wolves?

Now, after examining these three great topics, we can better see how essential it is to remain faithful to the nature of the Church, even if at this moment its unity is compromised by external elements. The best way to bring it back to the normality envisaged by its Founder does not lie in unprincipled yielding but in solid faith in the assistance from on High, even if at the present we seem to be reaping utter failure.

8

WHAT MUST WE DO?
GO BACK TO POPE
BENEDICT'S LETTER

Eighth Lecture
June 28, 2017

Let's look back at the last seventeen years
[2000–2017].

From the previous lectures you can see how,
after Cardinal Tomko, things in the Holy See did
not go too well for the Church in China. The
years of Tomko's successor resulted in a vacuum.
After him, the noncooperation of senior Vatican
officials nullified Pope Benedict's efforts to cope
with the Church's difficulties in China. The Chinese translation of the Pope's Letter was manipulated, and the impressive commission he set up
could not be fully effective. The Church in China

This lecture has been slightly modified and updated.

was gradually weakened: in the official community, opportunistic elements are increasingly numerous, while in the underground community the Bishops are becoming fewer and fewer. The Holy See advises everyone to give in to government authorities. At the same time, our government has become increasingly arrogant because it feels rich and powerful, and the Church has become an easy prey. Benedict was Pope, but the one Vatican official who negotiated with China was Monsignor Parolin. Together with the powerful Prefect of the CEP, he pursued a policy of Ostpolitik in which they had great faith. The commission for the Church in China was never informed of the progress of the negotiations.

A turning point

In 2009 the signing of an agreement that was said to be imminent unexpectedly vanished. We speculate that the Holy Father rejected it because it seemed to yield too much to the other party.

Parolin was consecrated Archbishop and sent as Nuncio to Venezuela. Savio Hon was appointed Secretary of the CEP. Shortly thereafter, the Prefect of the same Congregation retired. (Actually he should have resigned much earlier on health grounds, but he insisted on staying on until he was seventy-five.) In his place Archbishop Filoni became the new Prefect of the Congregation.

For many years, Monsignor Filoni was in charge of the Holy See in Hong Kong and knew very well the situation of the Church in China, which explains his position of firmness when he took office. In the two meetings of the Standing Committee, which he presided over, he told the members that a new strategy had to be adopted. Since the Holy See's tolerance and hope that the good Bishops in the official community could make a change from within had failed, now it was time to tackle the situation directly and let everyone know that for the Catholic Church, the CPCA is not acceptable.

He rightly foresaw that the government was going to respond harshly to our firm stand. Right away, he asked some of those present to write "catechetical" articles to prepare the new campaign. But the campaign was dead, even before it got started.

But a major turning point occurred: Pope Benedict resigned in February 2013; in the following March, he was succeeded by Pope Francis.

Pope Francis is a man full of love and has great compassion for the poor and the weak, but he has no experience of real Communism (in power). He knows the Communists of Latin America, where they are the voice of the people who have suffered persecution. Pope Francis naturally has a lot of sympathy for them.

Parolin, Secretary of State of His Holiness Pope Francis

The first thing that the new Pope had to do was to choose his Secretary of State. The choice fell on Pietro Parolin, who was recalled from Venezuela and made a Cardinal. Everyone applauded the choice because Parolin was regarded as a wise and courteous person, a tested diplomat.

I too was among those who applauded his appointment. But I was painfully surprised when he soon proved to be arrogant and despotic, interested more in diplomatic (worldly) success than in the triumph of the faith.

My first surprise came when, in a speech to commemorate his mentor, Cardinal Casaroli, he described the heroes of faith (Cardinal Wyszynski, Cardinal Mindszenty, and Cardinal Beran, without naming them) as "gladiators, people who systematically opposed the government, eager to show off on the political stage"! To despise these heroes is to despise the faith!

The other surprise came when he quietly made the commission for the Church in China disappear, giving up on the tradition of good diplomatic manners of the Holy See, even when they do the worst things. Obviously, he no longer had the patience to listen to my discordant voice.

This was followed by the cunning way in which Savio Hon was removed and sent away from Rome but kept in tight control, by making him an operative of the Secretariat of State.

But what worries me the most is his lack of respect for the truth. Intelligent as he is, the sophistry and half-truths (half-quotes) can only be willful lies.

An alarming situation

After getting rid of me (by removing the commission in China) and Savio, Cardinal Parolin had the whole field to himself, so to speak. He took Pope Francis down the slippery slope of his optimism. But Parolin knows very well the horrible face of Chinese Communism! Why does he hide the truth from the Pope?

When we meet friends in the media, we feel embarrassed when they mention the many things that make our "holy" See more and more ridiculous.

Father Lombardi, former director of the Holy See Press Office, always allowed Hong Kong's Phoenix Television to interview him. (Could he not find a neutral station at least?) They got a certain Sisci (who has, of course, now become a great personality) to interview the Pope, and the interview did not touch religion but culture. (What culture? That of feudal society, which the Communists have long since thrown out the window!) Then there is the great senior Vatican official Bishop Marcelo Sánchez Sorondo, who invites a criminal as a guest of honor to an organ transplant symposium, precisely the criminal who is under investigation by international experts for trafficking in organs taken from living people. He told the joke that made the whole world laugh: "China is the best implementer of Catholic social doctrine."[1] All this to please the Chinese and get them to accept a bilateral agreement.

We are kept in the dark and know nothing for certain. But the bits of information we have been able to gather do not reassure us at all.

My plea

On June 23, 2016, fearing that a "bad" deal could be signed soon, I issued a heartfelt plea to my

---

[1] " 'China Is the Best Implementer of Catholic Social Doctrine', Says Vatican Bishop", staff reporter, *Catholic Herald*, February 6, 2018, http://catholicherald.co.uk/news/2018/02/06/china-is-the-best -implementer-of-catholic-social-doctrine-says-vatican-bishop/.

brothers in China: "Stay calm. Don't panic. Let's keep our honor high! Don't let the opportunists say that we, as faithful defenders of the Pope's authority, have now become rebels."

So far, I have criticized the Holy See, because I learned with sorrow that the Holy See is not always the Pope. But if an agreement is signed, the Pope certainly consented. I will never lead a rebellion against the Pope; I will quietly withdraw to the monastic life of prayer and penance.

My plea continued, "For you, a new age of the catacombs will begin. It will be winter. It will be hard on you. The government will seize your churches. The priests will no longer be able to administer the sacraments. All that will be left for you is to go home to farm the land. But you will always be priests. Reassure the faithful that God's grace is not tied to the sacraments. God has a thousand ways of filling your heart with his grace."

I remember an expression that appeared a long time ago on a Catholic website in China: "For many years our enemies have failed to make us die. Now we have to die at the hands of our Father. All right, let's go and die."

Have you ever noticed that children, even when they are spanked by their mother, don't run away, but cling to her leg, crying and screaming, perhaps? They don't know where to go, far from their mother!

Will the Pope sign a bad agreement? Not very likely

Pope Francis has often praised martyrdom and has said that martyrdom "bears fruit, and what fruit!"

In Korea during the 2014 Asian Youth Day, Pope Francis spoke to Asian Bishops about dialogue and said: "The first principle of dialogue is coherence with one's own identity." This clearly states that the Letter of Pope Benedict (with its clear ecclesiology) is still valid!

At a personal level, the Holy Father has always showered me with tenderness. Once, in St. Peter's Square he came toward me, making the gesture of firing a pebble with a slingshot, and said: "Here's the one who goes into battle with the slingshot!" He compared me to David; that is a great compliment.

He granted me a private audience twice. Recently, betraying his confidence, I revealed in public what he had told Savio and me in private, but he did not reproach me; instead, he even told me that I am "a good man", "a little scared".

The ones we fear are Pope Francis' collaborators, infatuated with Ostpolitik.

What is Ostpolitik?

When the Cold War was raging, someone said, "The Communists are there, and we don't know how long they will be there. We cannot ignore them. We must engage them." Thus, the Chancellor of West Germany began a dialogue with East Germany (the new Eastern policy).

Now politics is about money and power. With these people we can negotiate. We can say that Ostpolitik was a success.

However, when the Church decided to adopt the same policy, what bargaining chip did she have to negotiate with the Communists? Not money. Power perhaps? What power? The spiritual power that Jesus gave to the Apostles? But that is not negotiable.

If we have this spiritual strength and keep to it faithfully, we must not be afraid. This is what we see in Vietnam. The Communists are communist there as well, but they do not have an association like the CPCA; the Church stands on her own, and the Bishops' Conference is still the true Catholic Bishops' Conference. There is talk of a "Vietnamese model", but I am told none exists. It is case-by-case. The well-rooted faith of the people manages to get good Bishops, despite the government's efforts to control everything.

I think this is something similar to what happened in Poland.

Unfortunately, when someone in the Vatican talks about the Church's "soft power", they still mean it in a political (worldly) sense. The gentlemen of the Vatican delude themselves if they think they are still among the "big players" in world politics.[2]

First of all, let's see if Ostpolitik was successful in the Church in Europe, as some claim.

When John XXIII and Paul VI allowed the Holy See to try this approach, the situation was impossible. The hermetically sealed "iron curtain" did not allow any information to leak out. Monsignor Casaroli was wandering in the dark. The commission of Cardinals was not able to provide him with any actual orientation; it gave him carte blanche.

At the same time, the Vatican was full of spies: from Poland, East Germany, and the Soviet Union.[3]

Casaroli was a saintly man, but he was no miracle worker. He humbly said that he sought only a "*modus non moriendi*" (a way of not dying).[4] The Church did not die because Ostpolitik saved it,

[2] See George Weigel, *The End and the Beginning: Pope John Paul II—The Victory of Freedom, the Last Years, the Legacy* (New York: Image Books, 2010).

[3] Ibid.

[4] See George Weigel, "The Ostpolitik Failed: Get over It", *First Things*, July 20, 2016, https://www.firstthings.com/web-exclusives/2016/07/the-ostpolitik-failed-get-over-it.

but because of the faith of those peoples (this is what Pope Benedict wrote to me one day).

But for Ostpolitik supporters, Casaroli succeeded in setting up the ecclesiastical hierarchy in those countries and thus guaranteed the sacraments! Yes, but almost all Bishops were backed by the regime. Given the strong faith of the people, even the servants of the regime could not and dared not destroy the Church. Unfortunately, Ostpolitik severely damaged the Holy See's credibility.

Gianni Valente almost wants to make us believe that Cardinal Wyszynski also admired Ostpolitik. How ridiculous!

So why did John Paul II make Casaroli his Secretary of State? Some say it was because the two had different ways of seeing things and so could complement each other, but there are also those who say that the Pope wanted to use Casaroli as a "smokescreen" so as not to scare the Russians and thus silently carry out his plan to free Poland and Europe from Communist dictatorships.

In order to know what Pope Benedict thought about Ostpolitik, just read that page in his "Final Conversations" (his interviews with the German journalist Peter Seewald after his resignation from the Pontificate), in which he clearly states that Ostpolitik was "a failure".[5]

[5] English version: Benedict XVI, with Peter Seewald, *Last Testament: In His Own Words*, trans. Jacob Phillips (London: Bloomsbury, 2017).

Ostpolitik in China

Unfortunately, in China the CPCA has succeeded; the Communists have managed to drive a wedge within the Church from the very beginning. Nevertheless, there were still so many healthy forces. Over the years, the Holy See encouraged compromise rather than supporting the brave.

Someone has called this compassion. What compassion? Encouraging people to accept slavery instead of getting rid of it?

Bishop Wu of Zhouzhi, who is recognized by both sides, wanted to prevent the government from organizing his episcopal ordination, imposing the presence of illegitimate Bishops. So, he had himself secretly ordained. Angry, the government refused to recognize him for ten years. In fact, they mistreated him. But in the end, with his clergy closely united, he was able to fulfill his pastoral duties.

Finally, the government said that if Bishop Wu accepted an invitation to concelebrate with the illegitimate Bishop Ma Ying Lin, then they would recognize him as Bishop. He agreed (we suspect with the Holy See's encouragement). From the pictures of that day, we can see that his priests, instead of looking happy, looked very sad. Why give in after so many years of brave resistance?

After five years of resistance, Bishop Thaddeus Ma of Shanghai wrote a "turncoat" article, going so far as to concelebrate with illegitimate Bishop Zhang Shi Lu in Fujian. There is a lot of speculation about what happened. But I doubt anyone will convince me that Rome did not suggest to him to make some conciliatory gesture. (The Vatican hasn't owned up to it, but neither has it denied it. It has simply said that being suspicious is not right.) But what have they gained? Bishop Ma has lost the trust of both the official and the underground communities. Five years ago [2012], the latter had pledged its obedience after Bishop Thaddeus Ma courageously quit the CPCA.

Dialogue

Realizing that the Ostpolitik was a failure does not mean closing the door to dialogue. Recently, Pope Francis said that "dialogue is a risk, but I prefer the risk than the certain defeat that comes without holding dialogue."[6] Quite so. Let us keep the door open to dialogue, but let us keep in mind its risks. What risks? Those of seeking an outcome at any cost. That of being deceived.

It is dangerous to start with the desire for an outcome no matter what. If the other party does

---

[6] Philip Pullela, "Exclusive: Pope Says China Talks Going Well, Dialogue Worth the Risk", *Reuters*, June 20, 2018.

not accept any compromise and wants us to give in completely, can we do it? No!

Sometimes we have to recognize that it is not possible to reach an acceptable outcome. If that is the case, we must humbly acknowledge the momentary failure of dialogue, hoping that in the future the situation might allow us to restart it. For the time being, let us do what we can— namely, strengthen the faith.

When we start from a position of weakness, we are already doomed to fail. All pacts at the end of a war are unfair because there are winners and losers. In recent years, the almost unrestricted desire for dialogue to reach an outcome has weakened our Church in China.

We cannot rule out the danger of deception. The Chinese are masters at playing with words. The gentlemen in the Vatican are no match. Moreover, for the Communists there is no truth; truth is what is needed for the success of the party.

On December 31, 2015, I wrote on my blog: "What will 2016 bring to the Church in China?" The doubts and anxiety of that time have not diminished but rather increased. Now I ask, What does the near future have in store for the Church in China? Once in a while, a chorus of elated voices tells us that a positive outcome can be expected from the long and arduous dialogue between China and the Vatican.

They admit that it won't be perfect, but it will give the Church some "essential" freedom. They say the cage will still be there, but we shall be able to have more room in it. They even say that a bad deal is better than no deal. This is absolutely incomprehensible!

To us, a terrifying scenario is unfolding, the sellout of our Church! There is no essential freedom but a semblance of freedom. Not reconstituted unity, but a forced cohabitation in the cage. From the point of view of the faith, we cannot see any gain.

The agreement appears to contain three parts:

1. The manner of appointing Bishops
2. The status of the seven "illegitimate Bishops"
3. The future of the "underground" community

Procedure for the appointment of Bishops

It seems that if we start with a "democratic election", then regarding the appointments by the "Bishops' Conference", the last word (how beautiful!) belongs to the Pope.

All this is phoney. There is no real election in China; everything is contrived, manipulated by the authorities. The Bishops' Conference "does not exist"; there is only the name. The government runs the Church (the official community), chairing the joint (farcical) meetings of the CPCA (a "patriotic association") and a Bishops' "Conference", both of which are stooges!

What good can come from such a mechanism? What last word can the Pope give? Can he approve? Can he veto? How many times can he veto before appearing unreasonable to the world?

In my opinion, it might be useful to apply to our case what the Hungarian theologian András Fejérdy said about the agreement between the Holy See and the Hungarian government: "For pastoral reasons—the full administration of the sacraments absolutely requires consecrated Bishops—, the Holy See viewed the completion of the Hungarian Bishops' Conference as so urgent that it accepted a solution that did not formally violate the canonical principle of free appointment, but in practice gave the Regime a decisive influence in selecting candidates."

Perhaps the only improvement over the present will be the reading of the Papal Bull, which will be allowed during the ordination; until now, it has been read in the sacristy before ordination.

The status of the seven "illegitimate" Bishops

Regarding the status of the seven illegitimate and excommunicated Bishops, including two who do not live in celibacy, Rome seems to be saying that all of them have already asked the Pope for his forgiveness and that once forgiven they can be recognized as Bishops. I never thought that we would reach such a level of contempt for the episcopal office!

How can we believe that they are repentant when, until recently, they committed countless acts of defiance vis-à-vis the authority of the Pope?

How dared they ask the Pope for forgiveness. Doesn't this mean that the government was wrong when it forced them to accept ordination? Isn't it obvious that for the government what is crucial is to have the Pope legitimize them? At that point, they will not feel in debt to the Pope but to the government, to whom they will be faithful and obedient.

Can such people be true shepherds? Has the Holy See forgotten the long lists Pope Francis made of the "required qualities" and "contraindications" for being a Bishop?

For Parolin, in five dioceses where there is no legitimate "underground" Bishops, the legitimization of the illegitimate is no problem. Unfortunately for him, two cases are a source of trouble because the Pope wants to avoid other Mindszenty cases!

The future of the "underground" community

It is said that the "underground" Bishops will finally be "recognized" by the government and will be able to join the Bishops' Conference. But how? By becoming members of the CPCA! What if, in good conscience, they don't feel like doing this? Will they be recognized as "emeriti"? How generous of the government!

With Vatican help, the government will have found the great solution (crushing the underground community); so, finally, there will be great unity! (Hallelujah!)

In a recent letter, I wrote to Pope Francis: "If the things that his" collaborators "are plotting become real, the consequences will be tragic and long-lasting, not only for the Church in China, but for the whole Catholic Church."[7]

Aren't the gentlemen in the Vatican saying that the purpose of an agreement is to favor the evangelization of the great nation? Let them remember that Communist power is not eternal! If today they go along with the regime, tomorrow our Church will not be welcome for the rebuilding of the new China.

[7] James Pomfret and Ann Marie Roantree, "Leading Asian Cardinal Calls for Vatican Foreign Minister to Resign over China Dealings", *Reuters*, September 20, 2018.

Right now, the whole world sees the state of religious freedom in China go from bad to worse. Can we hope to gain something from coming to terms with this government? When I say that it's almost like hoping that Saint Joseph can get something out of talking with Herod, I am not joking.

So what must we do? Let's go back to Pope Benedict's Letter, at the beginning of which he prays to the Lord, quoting Saint Paul, asking that "you may be filled with the knowledge of his will ... [and] strengthened with all power, according to his glorious might, for all endurance and patience" (Col 1:9, 11).

At the end of the Letter, quoting the First Letter of Peter (1:6), he wishes everyone to "rejoice", even "though now for a little while [they] may have to suffer various trials". And he asks that "Mary Most Holy, Mother of the Church and Queen of China, ... in the silence of hope ... intercede for all of [them], together with Saint Joseph and the countless Holy Martyrs of China."